A Fun & Care Book
CATS!

For Today's Pet Owner
From the Publishers of CATFANCY Magazine

Kate Zentall

photographs by Reneé Stockdale

BOWTIE™ PRESS

Irvine, California

Cover photograph courtesy of Robin Buckley

Ruth Berman, editor-in-chief
Nick Clemente, special consultant
Yumi Oshima, designer

The cats in this book are referred to as *he* or *she* in alternating chapters
unless their gender is apparent from the activity discussed.

Library of Congress Cataloging-in-Publication Data

Zentall, Kate, 1948-
    Cats! : for today's pet owner from the publishers of Cat fancy
magazine / Kate Zentall ; photographs by Reneé Stockdale.
        p.   cm. -- (A Fun & care book)
    Includes index.
    ISBN 1-889540-04-8
    1. Cats.   I. Title.   II. Series.
SF443.Z45   1998
636.8--DC21   97-32164
                                                                         CIP

BowTie™ Press
3 Burroughs
Irvine, California 92618

Manufactured in the United States of America

First Printing April 1998

10 9 8 7 6 5 4 3 2 1

Acknowledgments

Dedicated to the cats I've had—Snoopy, Cinnamon, Gypsy, and Soodie—whom I didn't know, listen to, or understand nearly well enough. And to the Maine Coon awaiting me—whom I'm more than ready for.

—K.Z.

I would like to thank the lovely librarians at the Fairview Branch of the Santa Monica Library, who kept on extending renewals on my reference books, and thanks to my adorable husband, Bill, who cut computer underbrush and tapped down a path—and kept watching to see that I was finding my way.

—K.Z.

To my son, Jerid. I am so proud of the compassionate young man you've grown up to be.

—R.S.

I would like to thank Sally Patch (Owl Cattery); Gary Smith (Orecreek Cattery); Micki and Kristin Burton (Pet Stop of South Lyon); Jo Anne and Tom White (Jo Anne's Place–Luxury Boarding for Cats); the Humane Society of Huron Valley, Ann Arbor, MI; and the great folks at Dr. Geake's Vet Clinic. I would also like to thank the models, human and feline, for their patience and hard work: Melissa Danley and Shadow; Robin, Jake, and Trevor Meinicki; Marti Jo and Myia Blackwood; Maximillian; Keli Quigley; Jan Grant; Amy McDonald; Dr. Lori DeGrazia; Dr. Kurt Henkel; Danielle Schreckengost and George; Beverly Peterson and Elliott. With Special Love to: Tigger, Punkin, Miss Bobbi Sue Varmit, Felix, Casper, Sweetie, Hairy, Lioness, Crickette, Chelsea, and all our foster cats and kittens and their adoptive parents. I would like to give extra special thanks to my husband, Gary, for building props, rearranging vacations, modeling, handling critters, and for his love and support of all of us.

—R.S.

Contents

The Cat in History

1

There are those humans who are immune to the charm of cats, and then there are those others who instinctivly fall under their spell or have given up any pretense of resistance.

Members of this last and privileged class have been graced over time with the company of this regal, congenial, loyal, ineffable, alternately wild and demure creature. They have been privy to how acutely in touch with the surrounding world cats are, not to mention how they are uncommonly intelligent, adaptable, cunning, and above all built for survival. This is a good thing, since the cat's history with our kind has certainly had its bumps in the road.

The Beginnings of a Wonderful Friendship

Evidence of cats and humans getting together goes back at least nine thousand years. Whether cats in these early rela-

tionships were pets or wild scavengers is impossible to tell. But even if people hadn't yet realized what wonderful companions felines could make, surely their value as mousetraps was appreciated. As humans in what is now North Africa and the Middle East began to benefit from growing their own food, and as they turned from nomadic hunting and gathering to ever more permanent settlements, they had to figure out how to store their food safely. Grain stores that made life in a village possible for groups of people were also a dream come true for rodents, and this posed a great problem.

Just like their wild ancestors, domestic cats today help keep barns free from rats and mice.

Enter the small wildcat. Hunting for food all day is a lot of work for a small predator in the wild, and stumbling on an exploding population of fat rats and mice in a human village must have been something else entirely. Suddenly, just by lingering near the grain storage, a cat could feast on a smorgasbord of rodents. And conversely, it couldn't have taken long for the settlement to realize that such creatures as these cats were not to be discouraged from hanging around. And so, with plenty to eat and no enemies willing to penetrate the cats' human protectors, cats were fruitful and multiplied. When, exactly, cats went from being merely tamed to fully domesticated household pets is impossible to tell, but a partnership was clearly born that would last and grow through millennia.

A Gift from the Gods

Cats helped protect the crucial Egyptian grain supplies along the Nile, were used in bird hunting and other sporting activities, and were thought to bring fertility to a family. It may be difficult for us, with modern pest controls, to fully grasp the importance of the cat to ancient peoples, but one indication is that cats were worshipped in ancient Egypt. By around 1500 B.C., Bastet, the goddess of love and fertility, was portrayed with the body of a woman and the head of a cat.

Eventually, cats became so revered that it was a capital crime to kill or injure one; in the event of a fire, it was decreed that cats were to be saved first. When a cat died of natural causes, his body first made the rounds of the priests, to assure that the death had been a natural one, and then the embalmers, where the body was mummified and prepared for sacred burial. The entire household, plunged into mourning, shaved eyebrows and otherwise publicly displayed signs of grief.

As civilization began to spread, so did the cat's popularity. Though it was forbidden to remove cats from Egypt, their value emboldened visiting Phoenician sailors to smuggle them out on ships trading throughout the Mediterranean. Though many cats were traded as exotic treasures, their usefulness on

Cat in Various Languages

- Felis . . . . .Latin
- Māo . . . . .Chinese
- Kadis . . . . .Nubian
- Qit . . . . .Arabic
- Gáta . . . . .Greek
- Katze . . . . .German
- Chat . . . . .French
- Gatto . . . . .Italian
- Gato . . . . .Spanish
- Kot . . . . .Polish
- Kóshka (also Kot) . . . . . .Russian

During the Middle Ages, people associated cats with evil and witchcraft. Superstitions, especially surrounding black cats, still exist today.

board ship wasn't missed by the Phoenicians, and the partnership of crew and cat was born. As centuries passed, the popularity of the cat continued to grow. The Romans took the first cats to Britain, and later the Crusaders brought home new varieties—longhaired Turkish cats and others—as part of the spoils of war.

Though cats were prized by returning warriors, the Middle Ages also saw fear, ignorance, and suspicion cloud the popular perception of cats. Connections between cats and witchcraft, as well as other superstitions, date from this time. Their nocturnal habits, silent movements, inscrutable nature, and sometimes eerie, humanlike cries in the night led people to associate them with the devil and other dark forces. The Church, disapproving of the cat's connection to pagan cults, took up this cry and embarked on an inquisition.

Certain calmer heads, meanwhile, recognized the cat's value in keeping down the rodent populations in the teeming towns and cities of the time—a time when bubonic plague, also known as the black death, raged throughout Europe. A household that included cats must have offered a better chance at skirting the ravages of a disease borne primarily by rats.

Nonetheless, for nearly a millennium, cats were cruelly persecuted, tortured, and reviled.

During the Renaissance, however, cats again got their due; from princes to peasants, there was hardly a family without one. The early colonists in the New World brought cats with them as valuable allies in their struggles against rodents, and as world trade expanded, cats continued to be an indispensable shipboard companion.

Today, passion for the house cat continues unabated. And while cats are not exactly sacred, they are nonetheless very much revered. To understand just how much, attend a local cat show, open the pages of any cat magazine, or stroll down the aisles of a pet supply store. Reflect on the fact that we spend more in this country on cat food than we spend on baby food, and consider that the total $2.3 billion we spend annually on cats exceeds the gross national product of many countries.

Or, with open mind and heart, simply observe one of these creatures stalking a venetian blind cord, getting intoxicated by a ball of yarn, or contemplating a housefly. Poised. Independent. Composed. Dangerous. Then watch him find and claim the warmest, sunniest corner of your home and surrender, coiled and unconscious, to the lull of its comforts.

Attitudes about cats took a turn for the better during the Renaissance. Now cats are pampered and loved in our homes.

The Nature of the Cat

2

A Growing Cat

What takes humans twenty or so years to achieve in development occurs in cats in just under a year. This accelerated cycle makes for a fascinating and remarkable relationship with any new kitten.

Kittens are born—an average of four to a litter—blind, deaf, helpless, and dependent. In this neonatal phase, their main concern is getting nourishment from their mother, who provides a warm, quiet, safe environment. They grow quickly. By about the tenth day of life (the transition phase), their eyes open, their first teeth come in, and they begin to stand and walk.

From week two to week fourteen (the socialization phase), full kittenhood commences. Let the games begin! Social play (with other cats), locomotor play (jumping, running, rolling,

climbing), and object play (batting, poking, tossing) head the activities. Depth perception at around four weeks enables a kitten to perceive where, say, the edge of a table is—though good sense won't necessarily keep her from plunging off. By six weeks, her balance is already better than ours. Weaning begins around this time. It is also the period of most intense interaction with other cats, and the time when good experiences with animals, including people, make the most indelible impression. By eight weeks, most all adult reflexes are functional, including the righting reflex that allows a falling cat to land on her feet. Adult sleep patterns are in place, and litter box etiquette is acquired.

In the next phase (juvenile), behavior and skills are modified and refined until sexual maturity, which occurs anywhere from four to ten months. An adult female can go into heat several times a year, and if mated she has a gestation period of about sixty-five days. If things go well, both male and female cats will live, on average, to be around fifteen years of age.

Wild Origins

The modern domestic cat, in all its breeds and varieties, is descended from a single species, *Felis sylvestris*. It was previously thought that several species—*Felis lybica* and *Felis manul* in particular—combined in various ways to produce the modern cat, but these are now regarded as subspecies of *F. sylvestris*.

The rugged but gentle Maine coon is a hardy cat who adapted to withstand the harsh winters of the northeastern United States.

In anatomy and behavior, cats are still very much akin to the faintly striped African wildcat they developed from thousands of years ago in the Middle East. The colors have changed a bit, but underneath they are essentially the same wild mousers that made them so useful to the ancient Egyptians. Nonetheless, over the centuries domesticated cats have come to breed faster (three cycles a year, as opposed to once yearly in the spring), and they are now slightly smaller with shorter legs. And since their diet is more varied and less carnivorous, their intestinal tracts are longer than those of their wild cousins.

Just how domesticated are cats, anyway? How far have we come from just taming them? The distinction is a fine one. Taming is merely the sufficient calming of a particular animal to allow human contact and interaction; domestication is a fundamental alteration of a species' disposition, physiognomy, or relationship to people that is passed on to future generations. A trained lion, for example, has to a certain degree been tamed. But it can hardly be said to be domesticated, and its progeny continue to be wild at heart. A house cat can be said to be domesticated because, despite the inherent wildness, the cat has changed and adapted and has handed down these adaptations to succeeding generations.

Kittens are not born knowing how to hunt. They may accept typical prey animals as friends, but being predators cats should always be supervised when around other species.

Wild Explanations of Cat Behavior

The behavior of pet cats has often confounded their owners—cats seem unpredictable, driven by unfathomable compulsions, and deeply connected to some inner agenda quite apart from our own. Yet most feline behaviors, stances, and even attitudes can be understood if they are seen for what they are: offshoots and adaptations of their fundamental, and not entirely shed, wild state.

The cat is a natural predator, and brain, body, and behaviors are built around that end. Cats are not born with the knowledge of how to hunt, though—hunting is learned behavior.

Kittens who watch their mothers hunt will be much better hunters than those who don't. Thus, many house cats have not developed the skills or the interest to hunt. Well fed and underschooled, a lot of housebound cats are a flop as mousers; the instincts are there—they'll still chase a ball of yarn—but the need and knowledge to chase down a meal are gone. But even if a cat is not a trained hunter, the residual hunting behavior is a big part of what makes cats fun to watch. They still stalk, pause, crouch, and pounce, even if it's only a dust ball they're after. To them, hunting is a sport, a pleasurable diversion, and a form of relaxation.

In the wild, however, the cat's hunting urge is in deadly earnest, with small rodents and birds the natural prey. And the competition for such tasty tidbits is intense, with birds of prey, canine predators, snakes, and other feral animals all equally interested in the same menu items. But cats have some great advantages: a tapetum lucidum, which allows for keen eyesight in dim light; extensive peripheral vision; and the uncanny ability to pick up the smallest movements. Cats have even uncannier hearing capability—five times better than ours, and with precision of exact location and special sensitivity to high-pitched (mouselike) sounds. Sharp, retractile claws, teeth designed for biting rather than chewing, an acute sense of smell, extraordinary reflexes and coordination, and the ability to move silently are all characteristics that help a cat hunt successfully. These features, plus excellent musculature, minesweeper-type whiskers that help a cat balance as well as identify what can't be seen, an astonishingly limber spine and flexible skeleton, and an awesome jumping mechanism that enables a cat to go from a standing start to five times her height with minimum effort, all equip the cat brilliantly for the contest. Even the cat's sleeping habits—sixteen or so hours of mostly light catnaps a day—are calculated to prepare her for sudden awakenings and short bursts of energy for high-performance sprints.

Most house cats with access to the outdoors sooner or later bring home a small, lifeless gift as a testament to their hunting nature and token of great regard for their owners. If you have

Whatever your cat may have learned, her physique and habits are geared toward making her a successful hunter.

any tact at all, you will accept such a tribute with grace—and dispose of the remains quietly and as soon as your hunter's back is turned.

The domestic cat, like all its relatives, is an instinctive, solitary hunter. Unlike dogs, cats do not form mutually supporting packs; they don't hunt or travel in groups. Cats sharing territory do establish a definite hierarchy.

Even though cats do not instinctively form packs, they can be socially complicated animals, using subtle body language and scent-based communication. Any cat allowed outdoors quickly finds herself involved with a neighborhood community of felines. The pecking order is definite, the rules firmly established. To become accepted into the club, any newcomer has to prove worthiness, and that may well involve a fight. At the top of the heap is the strongest and toughest of the unneutered males—the top tom. The other unneutered males are arrayed at various levels below. Any tom who wants to rise in status has to fight for it. Neutered males are at the bottom of the social ladder.

Cats physically establish their hierarchies. By providing various perches, you can help cats determine who's top cat.

Queens, unneutered females, have their own hierarchy, with the most fertile queen at the top. As with the males, neutered females occupy the lowest ranks. The top queen does not necessarily mate with the top tom. Queens in heat mate with males at all levels of the group. Perhaps this has to do with the sexual cycle of the female. While she is sexually active, a period of only a few days, she mates as often as she is given the chance. Within half an hour of one coupling, she is interested in mating again.

If the feline social ladder is not primarily about sex, then what? Territory. The territory of a dominant tom may be dozens of acres, that of a neutered female perhaps only an armchair, but all cats control some. A mother cat with kittens takes as much territory as she needs and fights fiercely to defend it. Multicat households have territories that overlap, and the shareholders often defend the areas together. A high-ranking tom may claim a lot of real estate but defend it somewhat loosely, and so on. Such staking out comes from a genetic directive to secure an area in which to hunt, feed, rest, and, most important to toms, mate—to pass on genes to the next generation.

And just how is this staking out accomplished? Cats have scent glands in their lips, chin, and forehead areas, and they mark their territory—including you—with them by rubbing against things. Hence the happy greeting we get as our cats wind around our legs, purring and rubbing in bliss at the reunion. Additional scent glands in the paw pads cause cats to mark still more territory by scratching. Our coarse human sense of smell cannot detect these subtle scents, but felines live by them.

And if a male cat has not been neutered, his definitive way of marking is to spray urine so strong smelling and unpleasant you never forget it. This underscores only one of many arguments in favor of neutering.

Many cats, especially unneutered male cats are compelled to mark their territories with strong-smelling urine.

But must every corner be spoken for? Not necessarily. To avoid constant conflict, cats set up communal areas where all can meet, plus pathways allowing access and free travel. Communal meetings seem to occur frequently, and not only when there is a sexually active female around. What purpose these gatherings serve is, for us, something of a mystery, but cats seem to delight in them.

Body Language

Body language is one of the clearest ways cats have of communicating, and they use posture, movement, and scent to this end. The tongue they speak is universal, with each part of a cat's body reacting differently depending on the situation being faced.

The defensive cat, for instance, arches her back and bristles her fur to make herself appear larger than she actually is; she opens her mouth and displays her teeth; her ears flatten and she lifts up and arches her tail. The purpose of this is to make herself appear as large and formidable a foe as she can.

The submissive cat does almost the opposite: she draws herself up into a tight, cringing position and wraps her tail tightly around her body. She flattens her fur, whiskers, and ears. By doing this, she's made herself as unimposing as possible: no threat to any attacker. "Just go away," she seems to say.

Even kittens employ body language.

The aggressive cat takes yet another posture: she crouches slightly, ready to strike. Her fur is smooth and her ears are back, with tail held near her body, possibly ticking back and forth. Her whiskers bristle and fan out, her mouth is open and curled in a snarl, and she emits a long, low growl. Stay clear; this one's ready to stand her ground. Each of these positions sends a clear and distinct signal to other animals, especially other cats.

When two adult cats meet for the first time, they approach each other with caution, tails whipping like metronomes, eyes fixed on the other. They may turn their bodies to fully display size and heft. One cat may get the message that she's outranked and then lower her tail and back, lay her ears sideways, and depart. Barring that, the two may get closer in their dance, even passing and circling one another, until the more aggressive one jumps to bite the neck of her adversary. A struggle may ensue, with interruptions as one cat temporarily withdraws to freeze in a submissive stance or else regroup to attack again. How the encounter plays out depends on each cat's motivation to be top cat.

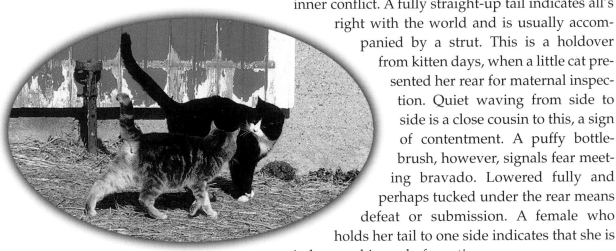

Once the hierarchy has been established, the dominant cat has preferential use of certain areas, toys, or resources and oversees how the other cats use them. Submissive cats defer to the dominant cat, and peace sets in.

If two submissive cats meet for the first time, the scenario differs to include careful sniffing around the face, flanks, and rear quarters, with tails up as a high-mast welcome. Face sniffing then leads to an exchange of scents from around the underside of the jaw in a rubbing action called bunting, which leaves scent marks by which cats can identify one another.

The tail is as good a barometer as any in sussing out what your cat is up to, and sometimes it's a dead giveaway of some inner conflict. A fully straight-up tail indicates all's right with the world and is usually accompanied by a strut. This is a holdover from kitten days, when a little cat presented her rear for maternal inspection. Quiet waving from side to side is a close cousin to this, a sign of contentment. A puffy bottlebrush, however, signals fear meeting bravado. Lowered fully and perhaps tucked under the rear means defeat or submission. A female who holds her tail to one side indicates that she is in heat and is ready for action.

These two cats have already established their hierarchy.

Tail held still but with tip twitching signals mild irritation. Measured, ticked-off wag: increasing annoyance. Lashing back and forth? Out-and-out anger. A few quick flicks up: "Hey, nice to see you!" The accelerating end-of-the-tail twitch, often accompanied by intensive staring, is usually inspired by the sight of real or imagined prey. And watch for wagging that falls between the serious and half-hearted; it usually involves an awkward decision to be made—as in wanting to go outside but knowing it's raining—and lasts until the conflict has been resolved.

Not only do cats have unbelievably acute hearing, but the ears themselves are of a wildly mobile nature, due to the more than twenty muscles that control them. Ears up and pointing slightly outward are a sure sign of confidence and relaxation; when they stay erect but turn forward, more alertness is indicated. Twitching nervously back and forth means anxiety or agitation. Flattened against the head more likely indicates

The flattened ears are a signal that trouble is brewing.

panic, defensiveness, or aggression. To the side and at half-mast means alert and defensive. Flattened down and sideways means more ambivalent—unless, that is, you're scratching the top of the cat's proffered, ecstatic head.

Feline eyes are a clear giveaway for what simmers within. A cat intent on intimidation employs a long, hard stare. This means that your own direct look at a cat who doesn't know you may be construed as a threat, which may explain why those very people who don't like or are allergic to cats are invariably the ones to whom a cat is drawn; these people don't stare at cats. In the context of other positive body language, however, a soft, head-on gaze can bespeak intimacy, acceptance, and affection, as can eyes that are narrowed into slits and punctuated by slow, happy blinks.

Dismissal, on the other hand, can be effected with a glance, a blink, and a turn away. Eyes completely closed can mean submission at the end of a cat-to-cat confrontation in which the retreating cat turns away from her aggressor in a gesture of self-protection, or, of course, the cat could be asleep. Wide, anxious eyes imploring a favor (open the door, feed me, toss me that catnip) challenge the most resolute owner—but this is not to be confused with the "Who, me?" look of wide-eyed innocence that invariably responds to an owner's discovery of disemboweled garbage or upset papers.

A cat's pupils themselves are often revealing. When a cat is greatly frightened or angry, adrenaline secreted during a "fight or flight" situation causes the pupils to enlarge; but this enlargement can also accompany a strong emotional response of the positive kind, as when contemplating a delicious bowl of food. Alternatively, a cat who is feeling aggressive may display pupils contracted into slits.

Other Forms of Communication

Kneading while purring is a sure sign of a content cat.

The great, hypnotic process of purring is one that belongs to cats alone, and only recently has it been fully understood thanks to the studies of Dr. David Rice at Tulane University. Once thought to come from vocal cords, purrs now have been found to result from vibrations of muscle surrounding the larynx. The resulting deep and throaty sound that people tend to associate with bliss is actually a more complex response that can be attributed to any number of stresses or even pain. Cats who are in labor, anxious about a vet visit, or badly injured have been known to purr long and loudly. Purring also serves an important newborn function: blind and deaf kittens can home in on Mama at mealtime with the help of those maternal vibrations, and then signal back that they're becoming satiated via the same communication—which, incidentally, not being a vocal process, does not interfere with nursing or sucking.

And speaking of nursing, those sharp little claws digging into your lap when your kitten or grown cat is blissed-out harkens back to a cat's nursing days, when such massaging at the breast brought the milk in. This kneading behavior, a sign of great contentment, may be accompanied by purring and even drooling, which is also associated with that early, mouth-watering activity.

Many of the common physical contacts between cats and their human companions are a replication of the contact between kitten and mother cat. When we adopt a young kitten, we take on the role of surrogate parents. When we lovingly stroke a cat, she feels much like a kitten being licked by her mother. The cat feels groomed, cleaned, and cared for. When cats rub up against our legs, often with the side of the head, they are exchanging scents with us; it is a way of bonding with us. As they subtly mark us with their scent glands and absorb our scent onto their fur, they are making us a part of their family.

Touching is an important part of the relationship between cat and human.

A Cat's Basic Needs

3

Cats are engaging and relatively independent, but it would be shortchanging any newcomer and the quality of your life together if you did not anticipate some of the very real needs this new companion will have.

A cat must be fed regularly with a healthy, balanced diet. The litter box must be kept clean. A cat needs you to train him to be responsible around your home. You, too, must adjust things around the house to protect your valuables as well as your cat's safety. There are visits to the vet, both regular (for vaccinations, boosters, neutering) and unexpected (for accidents and illnesses). Grooming is also important, especially with longhaired cats, to keep the coat healthy and attractive and free of fleas. And when you go on vacation, you'll need to make arrangements for his care.

By now it's probably becoming clear: A kitty's not a sometime thing. In fact, you can be certain that in the first few months, a kitty's sure to be a round-the-clock responsibility. Does this mean that that adorable, sweet, ingratiating, furry scamp will never sleep? It does not. But will you be able to anticipate when that sleep occurs? You will not. And between those naps, any self-respecting kitten will get into a good deal of mischief and require an equal amount of your supervision.

With a kitten around you can forget about reading a newspaper, making a bed, folding the laundry, sewing anything, packing anything, wrapping anything, trimming

Opposite Top: *Little kittens are a big responsibility and must be watched and protected.*

Opposite Bottom: *Getting your kitten used to being touched and having his paws handled while he's still young will make grooming later on a much easier task.*

Costs of Care

It is, of course, impossible to predict exactly how much your cat will cost you over the period of a year, or to anticipate what emergencies, medical or otherwise, may come up. Food alone, depending on the brand you and your veterinarian choose, can range pretty widely in price. During the first year, you can expect particularly significant start-up costs.

These figures reflect both a 1996 survey conducted by the American Pet Products Manufacturer Association and recommendations from pet supply stores, but costs in your area and your own spending inclinations may affect these projections considerably.

First Year or One-Time Expenses

Carrier	$ 5.99–30.00
Vaccinations	$50.00–80.00
Neuter/Spay	$20.00–80.00
Grooming	$31.00
Scratching Post	$14.00–20.00
Litter Box	$ 7.00–45.00

Annual Expenses

Food	$200.00
Flea & Tick	$ 50.00
Treats	$ 19.00
Litter	$150.00
Boarding	$ 12.00–30.00/night
Toys	$ 18.00
Vet Bills	$ 24.00+

anything, or writing anything without the tireless, wholehearted, and exasperating participation of your new friend, ever on the alert for any stray moment you may need for concentration, deliberation, or privacy of any kind.

Still intrigued? You've passed an important test. Read on!

Basic Grooming Starters

Just as a mother cat starts her ministrations early in a kitten's life, so should you lay the groundwork to make grooming a habit. Do this soon after your kitten's arrival to establish

a routine that will be followed by you and tolerated by your cat. Holding, petting, and playing with your pet at first will inspire trust and distract him from realizing that he is being restrained—a loathsome circumstance to any cat with an ounce of pride or sense.

In the beginning, take your time stroking gently and calmly in the direction the hair grows, running your hand down the tail, looking in the ears, lifting the lip. Apply a little pressure to the toe, unsheathing the claw. Speak soothingly and kindly, taking care to stop if the tail starts twitching or other signs of annoyance surface. As you're "playing," cradle the kitten gently but firmly with one hand under the chest, fingers holding front legs together, and hold the body close to yours. Accustom the kitten as well to being on his back—a submissive position his mother imposed on him for similar purposes that called for a real degree of trust. It comes in very handy in the grooming process. The same goes for playing gently with Kitty's paws, which desensitizes them for eventual nail clipping. Gradually add a comb to the proceedings, and try to find a regular time each day for your little session. Always approach a cat with gentleness and respect, and stand your kitten facing away from you when you brush his underbelly. Be especially careful around the animal's hindquarters.

Do not allow your pet to scratch or bite you, and if he escapes, go fetch him back and resume grooming. This is a good time to make clear that you are in charge and to correct bad behavior. When your session is over, you may want to reinforce good behavior with a treat reserved for just this time, especially in these early stages.

Before combing or brushing, physically "check in" with your pet and inspect ears, eyes, and claws. If the inner ear flap is dirty, clean it out with a ball of cotton dabbed with olive oil or an ear solution recommended by your veterinarian. Persistent scratching may indicate an infection or the presence of ear wax, though a honey-colored, waxy substance is normal.

Eyes should be clear and clean, but some longhaired and short-muzzled breeds get tear duct blockages that result in tear tracks down the face. Wash these with a cotton ball dipped in warm water.

Now the claws: Nail trimmers designed for cats do the best job of cutting your cat's nails. Press down lightly on the soft paw pads to expose the clear, hooked nails. Trim the clear, whitish tips only—never the pinkish quick, which hurts the cat. Weekly nail trimming helps control destruction if your cat claws or scratches in your home, but even with trimmed nails your cat will scratch the furniture and do some damage.

After checking your cat's eyes, ears, and paws, it's time to start on the coat. Cats in the wild shed hair in response to

Clipping your cat's nails isn't difficult once you learn how to hold the cat and work quickly. End your session on a positive note with a treat.

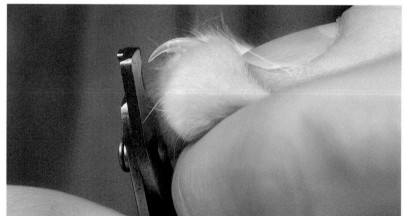

Declawing

Many uninformed people think that declawing is the only solution for a scratching cat. Declawing is done entirely for the benefit of the owner. There are absolutely no benefits for the cat. On the contrary, the procedure has been referred to as inhumane, mutilating, and barbaric.

The declaw surgery consists of ten complex, painful amputations, after which the muscles of the back, legs, and shoulders gradually weaken impairing the cat's balance. Moreover, in losing his claws, the cat loses a significant aspect of his line of defense, as well as a mode of expression. Unable to walk normally, his posture altered, the declawed cat is likely to feel more vulnerable and thus more stressed. Defensive biting may increase to compensate for the loss of claws, and a cat may bite more as an outlet for the tension and nervousness he may feel.

For some owners at their wit's end with a destructive or pain-inflicting or "untrainable" cat, declawing may be all that stands between that

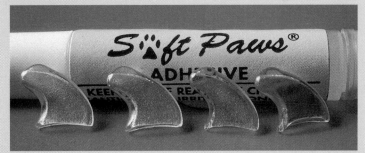

cat and the pound. Even people most opposed to the procedure admit that declawing is a better option than an animal shelter. To a person considering declawing a cat we can only offer reluctant advice to read up on it as much as possible, discuss it in depth with an experienced veterinarian known to have performed the surgery many times, and seriously consider whether you have indeed tried absolutely everything—claw-trimming, vinyl nail-caps, help with scratching-post training—and if you are ready for the personality changes declawing a cat may cause.

Certain people claim that once recovered from the procedure, their cats show themselves to be as affectionate, playful, and content as before. We cannot help thinking that this is the exception rather than the rule and emphasize that early training to encourage acceptable scratching habits be started as soon as a cat comes to live in your home. Given this positive alternative, there is little likelihood a cat will prove himself destructive enough to warrant your resorting to such extreme, painful, irrevocable measures.

increased daylight, such as during spring and summer. We have upset the natural order by keeping our friends indoors under artificial light, so shedding goes on all the time.

30

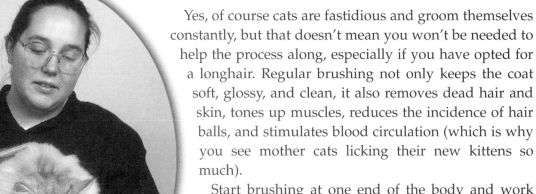

Yes, of course cats are fastidious and groom themselves constantly, but that doesn't mean you won't be needed to help the process along, especially if you have opted for a longhair. Regular brushing not only keeps the coat soft, glossy, and clean, it also removes dead hair and skin, tones up muscles, reduces the incidence of hair balls, and stimulates blood circulation (which is why you see mother cats licking their new kittens so much).

Start brushing at one end of the body and work your way around. Follow up with a comb to certify there are no tangles. Longhaired cats need two daily grooming sessions of fifteen to thirty minutes each (their beauty bears its own price) to avoid mats. Shorthairs require less grooming—only a couple of half-hour sessions a week—not only because their coats are easier to manage but because they have longer tongues than their longhaired relatives, making them more efficient groomers.

The Plunge

Many cats live happy, healthy, and fulfilled lives without bathing at all, and while your cat probably will not need frequent long hot soaks in a tub to soothe shattered nerves, the time may come when his coat will get dirty or greasy or need to be treated for fleas. So why not get a young kitten (but never one younger than four weeks) habituated to the occasional bath before he figures out he's supposed to hate them?

First, comb the coat out well. Then, making sure the room is warm and draft free, gently place the kitten in a rubber-matted sink (or one with a towel at the bottom)

filled with a few inches of warm water (some cats like to prop themselves up on the wall of the sink). Using a sponge, wet down the cat, then apply a special baby shampoo or flea control product specially made for cats or kittens. Some owners wrap a small towel around the cat and soak that with water, which more gently wets the cat. Lather, rinse thoroughly with either a spray attachment on a gentle setting or cups of water, then wrap your kitty in a large, warm towel. Fluff dry, with the help of a blow-dryer if your cat will tolerate it.

How often baths occur is completely up to you and

your cat. Supporters of baths recommend once a month or so, but to be perfectly frank, certain cat experts do not think of baths as a priority.

Fighting Fleas

You can check for fleas by turning a kitten on his back and parting the fur on his belly, which sends fleas in motion to get away from the light. You can also put the kitten on a white paper towel and briskly rub his fur, thus dislodging the flea dirt, which becomes visible on the paper towel.

No single flea control product works completely by itself; you must fight the critters on all fronts—cat, home, and yard. Most products for attacking this problem are not safe for kittens, so check the directions carefully. Keep in mind that a kitten with fleas may have tapeworm as well.

These days, many owners favor alternative flea control methods over insecticides. Health food stores and pet stores, as well as some veterinary hospitals, carry alternative flea collars, combs, shampoos, and dips containing aromatic oils that are gentler to an animal's system. In addition, some once-a-month flea prevention products have been developed. They are available nationally through veterinarians.

Washing and vacuuming rugs, furniture, and areas frequented by your cat will help control a flea situation, as will removing fleas from your pet with daily grooming using a fine-tooth flea comb—metal lasts the longest. Whatever methods you choose, be extremely cautious when using insecticides around your pets and your family; read all flea control product labels carefully; and use great care if combining insecticides—the combinations can raise dosages to danger levels.

Dental Care

By the time kittens are sixteen weeks old, they start losing their baby teeth and getting their adult teeth. By week twenty-four, they should have the adult set they'll be living with for all the coming years. Brushing your cat's teeth once a week with a soft toothbrush and pet-formulated toothpaste (never human kinds) prevents plaque buildup and gum inflammation, or gingivitis. Gauze wrapped around you finger and soaked in salt water, diluted hydrogen peroxide, or dipped in a paste of bak-

Opposite: *Longhaired cats require (at least) daily grooming sessions to keep their coats shiny and mat free.*

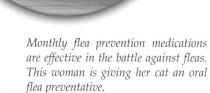

Monthly flea prevention medications are effective in the battle against fleas. This woman is giving her cat an oral flea preventative.

It's easier to brush a cat's teeth if you started his dental care while he was young.

ing soda and water also works well. It's important to start this ritual soon, not only for the sake of thoroughness but to get your pet used to it early.

Food

Before you bring him home, ask your veterinarian what foods and in what portions to offer your kitten, and stock up on a suitable supply. Opinions differ regarding canned and dry food. The advantages to dry food are that it can be left out without spoiling, and the kitten can eat what he needs when he needs it—though smaller allotments throughout the day of any food are optimal. Moist or semidry foods (those that come in foil packets) are convenient but tend to be high in preservatives, sugar, and salt.

Kittens in particular need food rich in high-quality protein. A dry kitten food (make sure the kitten's teeth are strong enough to crunch it) should contain at least 30 percent protein and 15 percent fat. Canned foods should have at least 10 percent protein and 6 percent fat, with moisture content not exceeding 78 percent. Kitten nourishment should also contain sufficient amounts of energy and fatty acids, so make sure animal fat (particularly poultry fat) is on the product list as well. Finally, the inclusion of vitamin A and taurine in the ingredients will ensure that your kitten gets all he needs. By the time a kitten is six months old, his declining energy needs may indicate he requires a different type of food. Check with your veterinarian.

If your new pet comes from a breeder, find out what foods the cat has been eating and when mealtimes occur. If you do change the type of cat food, introduce the new victuals gradually, mixed in with the familiar food, to make the adjustment less abrupt to the cat's system. Even changes in water can lead to gastrointestinal distress, so offer bottled water at first, then taper it into tap water. It helps, too, to avoid such hard-to-digest foods as raw eggs and cow's milk.

Use the information you get from books, magazines, and veterinarians to help you choose among the variety of bowls, foods, and treats that are available.

Use whatever dishes suit your needs or sense of aesthetics, as long as there is no lead content (as there is with some ceramic dishes made outside the United States). Lighter plastic or metal bowls are easy to clean but may be tempting for spirited kittens to spin and bat around. Heavier ceramic bowls and dishes, while breakable, are dishwasher and microwave safe. It's your call.

Whole books have been written about vitamin and mineral supplements to a cat's diet—just as they have about enhancements to our own diets. But before you consider these additions, know that virtually all commercial kitten foods already contain necessary vitamins and minerals in forms that can be easily absorbed by your pet. Know, too, that too much of a good thing can bring on problems. So in the beginning, at least,

34

hold off on the supplements—unless, of course, your veterinarian recommends them.

You'll be obligated to put out fresh offerings at least twice a day—more in the beginning, since kittens need frequent tank-ups. This process is not time-consuming as much as it is incontrovertible: Every day, come rain or shine, your cat will need to be fed. Twice. Every day.

Training

Getting your kitten accustomed and socialized to his household is very much an ongoing process, but your vigilance and attentiveness will be particularly important during the first few months. Putting in the extra time in the beginning will pay off later in good behavior and better understanding all around.

No kitten really needs to be trained to use a litter box if you provide one that is accessible and relatively private, but you do need to keep it pretty clean. This means scooping solid wastes and clumps daily and washing out the box twice weekly with a mild detergent and rinsing it thoroughly (cats hate soap smells and can be harmed if they pick up soap residue and ingest it while grooming). Should any accidents occur, thoroughly clean the area quickly to avoid any repeated offenses, since lingering scents draw the cat back.

Scooping out the litter box daily will keep both you and your cat happy.

Training a cat away from aggressive or destructive behavior is really a matter of seeing to it that such appropriate outlets as scratching posts and toys are available and being used, and by putting in a little time to out-and-out play with your wild, hedonistic party animal, using appropriate toys in appropriate ways. Never allow your fingers, hands, or feet to be grabbed, pounced on, or batted at, making the parent-approved offerings all the more enticing because they involve . . . you.

When You Go on Vacation

Sooner or later there will come a time when you have to leave town and you can't take your friend with you. The separation will be made a lot less disturbing for both you and your cat if you've done a little homework and decided on who'll be caring for your charge, and where.

Kennels are becoming an increasingly popular option, and some newer, enlightened facilities offer wonderful, heavenly environments. They may offer private rooms, sheepskin beds, climbing poles, nutritious food, kitty videos, exercise play-rooms, extra playtime, and carpeted window ledges facing bird feeders, squirrels, and woods—in short, the works—for around $10 to $15 a day, and up to $30 in large urban areas. If you're lucky enough to have access to one of these facilities, chances are your cat will have at least as good a time on his "vacation" as you will on yours.

Many provisions and stipulations can be found in the board-ing contract; study it carefully before signing it. Experts also recommend that you play it calm and cool when dropping off your friend; emotional good-byes do not reassure your cat of your affection and only create more anxiety.

The least stressful solution in almost all instances is a loving, dependable cat-sitter, someone who can come to the house to care for and play with your cat in his familiar environment. This spares the cat the trauma of being moved to another, unfa-miliar place, or of being exposed to other animals and any

Scratching posts and toys will help keep this cat from climbing the drapes.

Some kennels create loving and toy-filled "retreats" for cats with people on the go.

Boarding Facilities

Keep the following questions in mind when you check out any boarding facility.

- Is the place clean and well ventilated?

- Is it completely secure?

- Are there at least two doors between your cat and the outside?

- Is proof of up-to-date vaccinations required?

- Is the place regularly exterminated for fleas and ticks?

- Is the place well supervised, day and night?

- Is the staff trained in animal care and medical treatment?

- Are the rooms or cages big enough for your cat to stand up and stretch out?

- Are there opportunities for exercise?

- Is a veterinarian on the premises, or at least on call?

- Is grooming, bathing, or training provided?

- Are other kinds of animals boarded, and if so, are they kept away from the cats?

Pet-Sitting Organizations

National Association of Pet-Sitters
1200 G St.
Washington, DC 20005
(800) 296-PETS

Pet-Sitters International
418 E. King St.
King, NC 27021
(910) 983-9222

inconvenient diseases or conditions they may carry. Creatures of habit, cats appreciate staying on home turf, and being the relatively self-sufficient creatures that they are, they should be happy with two visits a day for a limited time. The added advantage of this arrangement is having someone who can also take in your mail, water your plants, turn lights on and off, check your answering machine, and keep an overall eye on your place.

How to find a cat-sitter? Start with the people already in your life whom you trust and who know your cat. Barring that, ask your veterinarian, groomers, the local humane society, and other cat owners for recommendations or organizations specializing in pet-sitters. If you're given names of professional cat-sitters, follow through with calls to the Better Business Bureau and Department of Consumer Affairs. Check, too, if the sitter is bonded, and ask for references, especially professional ones.

Make sure the sitter likes cats, knows how to handle them, and is familiar with the tenets of cat proofing, as well as the signs of illness. Set up an interview well before your trip. Watch the interaction between sitter and pet. Unless your sitter is completely familiar with your cat's innermost habits, prepare a list detailing his routines, preferences, and schedules. Include the number of feedings, kind of food, how often to change litter, grooming requirements, favorite toy, and so on. Point out where you keep the carrier, food, and medicines, as well as light bulbs and fuses, and how your heater and air conditioner work. Include your veterinarian's phone number, your itinerary, and a local emergency number of anyone who knows your cat well. Be very clear about what, exactly, the sitter will be responsible for, and work out the financial arrangements ahead of time. Fees vary wildly, of course, depending on where you live, who has been hired, and what duties are assigned, but $10 to $25 a day is not unusual.

Some owners leave special treats for the sitter to dispense while they are away, as well as a small pile of dirty laundry bearing their scent. But no matter how well your cat does while you're away, or how nicely he plays with the sitter, don't be surprised if you get some attitude when you return. This is normal. And temporary. Most cats can't maintain the charade for long and are soon back in your lap, a-purring—probably just when you need most to get up.

Your cat may play it cool when you first come home from a vacation, but he won't be able to keep it up for long.

Finding the Right Cat for You

4

Cats may well be the ideal all-around pets—after all, as many as 64 million of them currently occupy a place in the hearts of U.S. owners—but taking one under your roof for fifteen years or more represents a substantial responsibility and commitment.

The most delightful, most heart-stopping kitty grows up—and quickly—into her own mature self, complete with idiosyncrasies and inconveniences, fleas and fur balls. Like a child, a cat will surely cramp your style a little, test your patience, and need feeding, cleaning up after, grooming, vaccinating, and disciplining, especially at first and undoubtedly at inconvenient times.

But in return, you get a friend for life—a challenging, amusing, sensitive cohort, a fascinating combo of demure puss and

independent creature of the wild. Cats can be content in limited space, and with your companionship they can thrive in small apartments. The busy person who finds it burdensome to spend time exercising a dog, for instance, may find that a cat's needs are less imposing. Many people who are elderly or disabled find the ease of care and loving companionship of a cat to be a great joy. Anyone taking the trouble to give a cat the amount of care and affection she requires will find that affection returned many times over.

Cats and Children

What about children? Cats and kids have been known to cohabit peacefully, but a fair amount of education and supervision are required on the part of an adult. Children may have every intention of being good caretakers, but they cannot always follow through. Furthermore, they may not realize how overhandling or teasing can hurt a cat—or even if they do, may not be able to control their wilder impulses. Children—and even some well-meaning adults—may maintain that having a cat will teach responsibility. But they cannot possibly know just how dependent a small cat can be, or what demands will be made on them and their time. Unless an adult is willing to take on overseeing the care of that cat, such an impulse may prove ill-fated. Whatever is finally decided, both adults and children would be wise to remember that cats are not toys, mascots, cute surprise gifts, or rewards.

Cats can become best friends and partners in crime with other household pets—especially if they are raised together.

One Cat—or Maybe More?

If one cat is great, are two twice as great? Sometimes. Maybe. Consider the size of your home, the number of people living there, whether your schedule allows you time to be home much, whether you have other pets, and whether your circumstances require a pet to be confined indoors.

A solitary indoor cat in a household where no one's at home much and where no other pets are around to keep her company is sure to be lonely. A single cat in a bustling, multi-pet household with adults and children coming and going throughout the day is likely to be perfectly content. Contrary to popular myth, cats are not all that aloof and independent; they really do need companionship of some kind if they are to remain healthy and happy. Dogs and cats have been known to cohabit quite successfully—as have cats and cats.

A single cat is certainly easier to train than two or three; when there is a problem, you know who the culprit is. The affections of a single cat will be yours and yours alone, while two may find all the company they need in each other. One compromise, if you hanker for more than one cat but don't want the stress of multiple kittens, is to intro-duce them one at a time. Once a sin-gle cat has had a chance to adapt to the household and learn its routines and expectations, as well as build a good relationship with you and oth-ers in the home (for a kitten, this takes about a year), another cat or kitten can be added with a modicum (well, depending on whom you ask) of trouble.

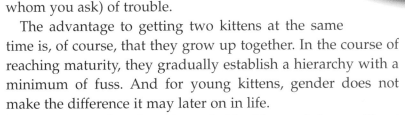

Two romping kittens keep each other from getting lonely.

The advantage to getting two kittens at the same time is, of course, that they grow up together. In the course of reaching maturity, they gradually establish a hierarchy with a minimum of fuss. And for young kittens, gender does not make the difference it may later on in life.

A kitten introduced to a household with an adult cat will not challenge the existing order the same way another adult would; as in most species, young cats display behaviors that signal their immaturity to adults, thereby assuring those pre-viously established citizens that the newcomers pose no threat.

What Kind of Cat?

Longhaired, shorthaired—or no hair at all? Yes, there are actually such creatures as hairless cats, genetically engineered creations of humans who make lovable, active companions—though they must never be left to their own devices outdoors. No coat means no insulation—but also greatly fewer fleas, no brushing, and often no problems for people with cat allergies.

Longhairs are magnificent and lush and lovely but require serious grooming upkeep that varies with the length and texture of their coats. Shorthairs are the most common and easiest to maintain.

Before choosing your cat, gather a little knowledge of the various breeds and their traits. Even if you decide to adopt one of a mixed breed, knowing something of the general habits and dispositions of the cat's lineage may guide your decision and help you arrive at the best possible match.

Nearly forty breeds are recognized among feline registry organizations in North America. These cat associations register kittens, oversee the standards of breeds, and decide which breeds and variations within breeds are recognized. Despite some differences between countries, particularly when it comes to the acceptance of new varieties, there is a general consensus worldwide.

Whether purebred or not, cats of varying colors, sizes, and coat lengths can be found.

Breeds are grouped in two broad categories: longhair and shorthair. The first domesticated cats are thought to have developed from African wildcats, who had short hair. They formed the basis for domestic cats throughout the world, and today their genes are still dominant over those of the longhairs. Either through spontaneous mutation, interbreeding wildcats with longer-haired cats from Russia or Asia Minor, or as an adaptation to natural conditions, longhaired domestic breeds began to show up in western Europe in the late 1500s. The longhaired varieties were the first pedigreed cats; pedigreed shorthairs are a comparatively new concept. Altogether, there are hundreds of different color varieties within breeds of pedigreed cats. They break down into five basic types: Persians, other longhairs, British shorthairs, American shorthairs, and Oriental shorthairs.

The whole concept of selectively breeding cats is relatively new, since they have been bred selectively only since the late 1800s, when the first cat shows piqued people's interest. Most variations in breeding have to do with color, pattern, and texture of coat. As for size and shape, cats are remarkably similar.

Cat breeds are not true strains in that they don't necessarily transmit their traits generation after generation (which is why breeders are so vigilant in trying to keep up certain characteristics they prize in their cats). For example, the Manx does not always pass on its taillessness.

Breeds also do not necessarily derive from the places their names suggest. There is no proof that Abyssinians, for example, are of Ethiopian origin, and Persians are more likely to be found in Russia than in Iran. In fact, most of the more established breeds were started only at the end of the 1800s and beginning of the 1900s, despite hints to the contrary and various exotic implications.

Is a purebred cat for you? Purebreds can be stunning, but are you ready for the extras involved? For starters, a pedigreed cat can be expensive—from around $350, but as much as $500 or more—and more susceptible to health problems due to the inbreeding that made them the grandiose creatures that they are. As a financial compromise, many people who are drawn to a certain breed find great satisfaction in less expensive "pet-quality" animals—normal, happy purebreds who may not meet a breeder's exact specifications for a show cat but who bear the traits that are so endearing to their kind.

Not all Scottish folds have the characteristic folded ears. It doesn't matter; folded ears or not, Scottish folds are still good-natured cats who make excellent pets.

Where to Go to Adopt Your Pet

So you've decided to bring a cat into your life and heart! Now for the fun: finding your new companion. Just where to go depends on what sort of animal you're after. If you want a purebred, seek out a breeder who will be able to ensure you're getting a healthy candidate and will provide papers for her. If it's a mixed breed you have in mind, many more options abound. But proceed with caution when approaching these options, which may include pet stores, ads, or the box o' kittens in front of the supermarket. You may find yourself taking on more than you bargained for. A cat of questionable origin may make a perfectly wonderful pet—most do. But a cat from a safe and happy environment, born of a healthy mother, is that much more likely to reflect those positive conditions. It all comes down to giving both you and your cat the best possible start.

Responsible breeders breed for only two reasons: to make certain their breed does not become extinct and to perfect the breed. A good professional breeder not only has the purebred of your dreams, should that be what you have your heart set on, but has a stake in the health and welfare of each cat produced. Most breeders have started inoculations and are able to guarantee a cat free of disease. Moreover, responsible breeders insist that buyers neuter their cats to prevent overpopulation and careless breeding.

Seek out a reputable breeder through local cat clubs, breed ads in cat magazines or local papers, through one of the many cat associations in the country, or from current owners of purebred cats who can tell you where they found their cats. Breeders can also be found at cat shows, though you will probably want to select your kitten from her home environment with the rest of her litter, away from the brouhaha of a show. The cattery should look clean and smell clean, the cages should be well sized, the litter pans clean, the water bowls full. If all is

Reputable breeders, such as this breeder of Burmese cats, provide each buyer with a health guarantee and any appropriate papers regarding the kitten's lineage.

as it should be, the cats are groomed and alert and friendly, especially to their current owner. And that owner will probably ask you questions too, making sure you and her purebred are in fact meant for each other, and that you will provide her with a good home.

Good pet shops have healthy animals and guarantee that you can return a chosen pet if this turns out not to be the case. Not-so-good pet shops can be breeding places for disease. Moreover, some pet shops buy their animals from kitten mills, which are often inhumane factories that keep caged cats for the

Pet stores (left) and animal shelters (below) are places you can go to choose a cat or kitten.

sole purpose of reproducing and nothing more—reducing the animals to so much collateral. Conditions can be miserable, and disease and injury rates high. Approach a pet store with caution.

Cats from private homes stand a good chance of being healthy, and the classified sections of newspapers are usually filled with ads for such animals up for adoption. If you're not looking for a show cat, a home-raised kitten is a promising candidate.

Most cats available for adoption in shelters are in good shape (for the simple reason that only the best, healthiest, and most adoptable are permitted to live). Humane shelters have all kinds of special breeds in the offing, in addition to endless varieties of mixed breeds. When you consider the millions of cats who are euthanized every year because there are no homes for them, the millions more awaiting in cages, and the millions who are suffering from neglect, malnutrition, and starvation on the streets, it makes sense to save a life while you're at it. So if you can, get your cat from a shelter.

Just Who Will this Creature Be?

Anyone who claims all cats are fiercely independent has clearly never owned a young kitten, who is primed for bonding with you. Cats, like people, are profoundly affected by the environments they're raised in and the way they are related to. Although each cat has a unique temperament, most are likely to adapt to the expectations they encounter in their new home.

Because cats go through all four major stages of development—newborn; transition; imprint (socialization with animals or people); and juvenile—at such an accelerated pace of twelve months or so, each week becomes particularly important in determining the sort of pet your cat will become.

For the best possible start, experts recommend bringing home a kitten anywhere between eight and sixteen weeks of age. Too much earlier, and she wouldn't have sufficient time to interact with siblings—a crucial developmental stage that teaches her to interact with other animals—and she would miss crucial mothering time (humans are unsuitable substitutes). Much later than sixteen weeks and a kitten would establish relationships according to the roughhouse rules of her littermates, making it harder to bond with humans.

These kittens (above and below) are at the perfect age for bonding with new families.

And yet, for every rule there are exceptions. Many a cat raised away from humans and brought into a household from the wild nearly beside herself with fear has, in the space of a few months, overcome her shyness and timidity to become as loving and responsive as any lap cat. A cat lover will find that patience and kindness can work wonders with all but the most scarred or tormented individual.

A kitten, adorable as she may be, requires a lot more from you those first few months than an adult cat. So if you must be out of the house a lot and expect to leave a new pet largely to her own devices, a mature cat may be a more appropriate choice.

Male or female? There are few generalizations one can make about gender, except that male kittens may be more active than females and that males tend to grow larger. But since you will probably neuter your cat whatever the sex, specific gender characteristics will be modified anyway. You may find yourself drawn, for some particular reason, to one sex or the other. Follow your instincts on this one.

You may be harboring a romantic notion—not unlike that enchanted evening when you'll spy the stranger you're destined for across a crowded room—that when you see the cat you're meant to have, you'll just . . . know. And sometimes in life that sort of thing does happen, and when it does it's magic.

But be wary of expecting your future companion to leap right into your arms and turn her face up to yours adoringly before introductions are even made. Remember, a cat may be so distracted or frightened or shy or confused in those first moments with you that she may not be as receptive as you had anticipated. When it comes to judging and assessing behavior, try to consider what the kitten or cat herself might be feeling when she meets you. Give the cat a little time. Then, if there is chemistry, you can ask the breeder, store owner, or shelter worker for more information about the cat you're attracted to.

Try to observe a kitten with her mother and littermates; much can be learned about a cat's personality in that context. Is the mother a "people" cat, who has passed on her own positive responses to her babies? Research shows that friendliness can be genetic as well as learned. Pick up (with care and respect, of course) a kitten you're interested in and see what happens. Is there a struggle, or does purring commence? When you put her back down, does she dash away fearfully or sniff curiously around the nearby territory? A kitten who's alert, friendly, playful, and outgoing and who can hold her own with a stranger is a good bet.

The bolder, bigger, and more forthcoming kitten may signify a sturdier—but possibly aggressive—model, while a smaller and more retiring sibling could be easily frightened, sickly, and less hardy. There are too many exceptions, however, that challenge the rules. This man's "sweet" is another's "wimpy"; that woman's "spunky" is another's "stubborn"; and one person's "full of life" observation can end up another's "drives me nuts" conclusion.

You can judge a kitten's temperament by watching her play with her littermates.

Health Signs

Unless you are adopting a cat in need or rescuing a creature under duress, you are most likely in the market for a healthy specimen, so always study a prospective pet's condition carefully. Do not let anyone talk you into taking a sick cat or resist your efforts to check out a new pet thoroughly. Take your time and move slowly so as not to frighten the cat. A short playtime before the inspection will put you both more at ease. While you're at it, watch for any limping.

Having your kitten's medical records will help at your first visit to the veterinarian.

Wherever you get your cat and from whomever you get her, ask what shots or boosters your new pet has received, and get hold of any available medical records. If possible, find out if the litter she was born into was healthy. Is the mother healthy? How long is the cat's health guaranteed, and what, exactly, is covered? Has the stool been tested for parasites, and if so, what were the results? Have both parents tested negative for feline leukemia virus?

Other questions to ask: What kind of cat litter has the cat been using (ask for a small amount to tide you over in case you don't have a chance to pick up the very same kind on your way home)? What food has she been eating? Can you get a sample of that, too? How long has she been weaned? In the unlikely event that things don't work out, is there a "return" policy? Finally, are there any idiosyncrasies it would help you to know about?

Cats and the Law: Your Rights

To any cat owner with heart or sense, a feline friend is a member of the family—even, to a degree, an extension of him or herself. The law, however, hasn't always seen it quite that way; legally, a cat has been considered personal property, pure

You should look for these healthy signs when shopping for a cat:

🐾 Coat is shiny, smooth, unmatted, and free of fleas.

🐾 Ears are clean and dry with no wax in them.

🐾 Eyes are clean and bright; the nictitating membranes, or third lids, should not protrude.

🐾 Nose is damp.

🐾 Mouth and teeth are pink and white, respectively—no inflamed gums.

🐾 Anus is clean with no sign of diarrhea.

🐾 Belly is rounded, but not hard, and free of hernia lumps.

and simple, an item whose worth is all too often reduced to its "fair market value," or cost of replacement. Sound unfair, inhumane, outdated? A New York court thought so recently, when it ruled that cats are more than inanimate objects because they receive and return affection so they hold a special place somewhere between personal property and a person.

This thinking may well continue to influence the law to protect cat owners and assure compensation beyond fair market value should your pet be wrongfully injured or killed. In some states, cat owners may be entitled to recover noneconomic damages for wrongful loss or injury. This means some form of compensation for emotional distress, loss of a cat's companionship, and annoyance or inconvenience resulting from the loss. While nothing can ever replace a beloved pet, such settlements are the law's attempt at compensation and should be taken as a legal nod acknowledging what most of us have known for a long time: that cats are hardly paperweights, espresso machines, or tennis bracelets.

The other side of this cats-as-consumer-goods coin is the protection it affords you, the consumer, should a pet you purchase turn out to be something different from what you pay for. For example, you buy a purebred Siamese cat who turns out not to be quite so purebred. Can the breeder be held responsible for breach of contract and violation of the consumer protection law? Yes, indeed. And if you buy from a cattery a healthy kitten who turns out to be diseased, you are also protected by your state's lemon law, which will most likely offer you several options ranging from getting a refund to being compensated for veterinary expenses. Moreover, a breeder's deliberate misrepresentation or false advertising can result in certain civil penalties, reimbursement of your attorney's fees, and other damages. This consumer protection extends to contracts for boarding, veterinary treatment, grooming, and even the sale of cat food.

So take heart. Laws regarding cats are evolving not only to protect you better but to support and acknowledge the place cats have in our families and lives as well.

Cats are more than just living property—they are affectionate family members who touch our lives.

Preparing Your Home

5

If you've never had a cat before, you'll want to make sure you have what's needed to make the transition smooth and joyous. When you think about it, it's not all that different from having a layette prepared for a new baby. Don't worry, you don't need all that much; you just don't want to get stuck without the necessities. And you'll want certain accessories at hand to get an early start with good grooming habits.

The essentials for a new cat include a carrier, litter box and litter, a collar and tag, food, dishes, grooming tools, and a bed. A carrier is absolutely essential. Because cars (or, for that matter, buses or trains) are not safe places for young cats to do their exploring, a carrier is a must—not only for the first trip home but for future visits to the veterinarian or groomer. The latest sturdy plastic containers can hold a cat comfortably, accommodate a car seat belt, provide safety in the event of an accident, and are acceptable for airplane cargo travel; some see-through models even come with a raised seat to provide a view. Soft-sided carriers often have zippered tops and ends, making it easier to get your cat in and out of them, and they are also easy to clean.

Before your new cat is even under your roof, make arrangements to get a tag engraved with your name and phone number on it, and then attach it to a breakaway collar that will slip safely off a kitten's head should it get caught on something. Put them on your new cat before you go home. As the kitten grows, check to make sure you can slip two fingers between the collar and neck.

Litter Box

The litter box is probably the one item you and your cat are likely to be most intimately associated with, so it bears a certain consideration in the choosing. Pet supply stores offer different models of litter boxes, and the one best for you depends on where you will put the box and how you prefer to monitor

There are a variety of litter box styles for you to choose from, and…

it. Small plastic bins are easy to clean and convenient when space is an issue, but an enthusiastic cat pawing and scattering the litter can quickly make a mess. Covered litter boxes are larger, help contain odor and litter, and even offer a little privacy. Some come with hinged lids to facilitate scooping; others have a sifter tray for easy disposal of solids.

In the beginning at least, try to use the type of litter (clay, newspaper, pellets, granulated) the kitten or cat is accustomed to for the sake of a less stressful adjustment. If you decide to

…there are many types of litter on the market.

change types of litter, mix in a little new with the old on a regular basis over a period of a month or so. Studies have shown that most cats prefer soft-textured, fine-grained litters.

As soon as you get home, place your kitten or cat inside the litter box. Between the excitement of all the changes and the length of the journey, the facilities will probably be used in short order. Having several litter boxes in different areas of the house will cover your bases at first, since very young cats are not always good at planning ahead. Make sure, too, that the sides of the box are low enough to permit easy access. Many owners restrict new kittens to one small room at first, so as not to overwhelm the newcomer with having to navigate a whole household. Once you decrease to one box, keep it in the same place—out of the flow of traffic and away from drafts.

Grooming Devices

To keep your cat's coat in top condition, you'll want to purchase a supply of grooming tools. You'll need a fine-toothed flea comb—metal lasts the longest—not only to extract fleas but to weed out loose hair, which a cat ingests during grooming and regurgitates as hair balls. Brushing regularly with a wire slicker brush or rubber grooming mitt stimulates blood flow, distributes oils, and keeps the coat shiny. It's also a good idea to purchase a soft toothbrush, cat toothpaste, and a pair of cat nail trimmers.

Depending on your cat's coat length and thickness, you will need a variety of grooming tools, including nail clippers.

Indoors or Outdoors?

A generation or two ago, the question of keeping cats indoors or letting them out probably would not have come up. It was a matter of convenience and largely the cat's prerogative. Not anymore. These days, between cars, poisons, insecticides, predators, and new feline-transmitted diseases, it is, more and more, a jungle out there. And so, overwhelmingly, cat experts are now advising that cats be kept indoors. While there are exceptions, cats have been known to lead longer, healthier lives indoors than when allowed out.

You need to weigh the pros and cons to determine whether you want to keep your cat indoors or allow him to go outside.

Those who favor allowing their cats the run of the outdoors speak of the advantages of not having a litter box to contend with and the obvious enjoyment cats take in climbing trees, playing in and gnawing on grass, sitting in the sun, chasing small living things, and running full throttle. Some people spend a lot of time outdoors themselves and appreciate having their cats with them. Neutered pets, they point out, rarely wander far from their own yards, appear regularly at mealtimes, and spend the night indoors. Indeed, it may be possible to achieve this ideal arrangement. But it's a gamble. And in the vast majority of situations, the risks posed by the outside far outweigh the advantages.

Isn't it cruel, some wonder, to confine such an active and curious creature, descended from a wild animal, to the inside of a home? Don't cats need space to exercise their instincts? Aren't they at home outdoors, designed to thrive outside? Perhaps. But remember, nature is brutal; there is nothing romantic or gentle about it. The life span of animals in the wild is short and favors only those in peak condition; even the fittest fall prey to disease, predators, starvation, parasites, and poachers. Sound like an overstatement when talking about a house cat in the backyard? Consider some of the hazards facing a kitty on just the back porch: dogs, poisons, diseased rodents, wild animals, chemicals, stray cats, sick cats, and angry neighbors.

If you think the dangers on the back porch are sobering, consider what awaits on the street. The automobile poses the greatest threat to most outdoor cats. Three cats are killed by cars to every dog, but the dangers extend beyond being struck. Cats can crawl into engine compartments for warmth and be killed or injured by the fan blades when the car is started. Open garages offer attractions to a curious kitty, but they can be lethal if the door is shut, trapping the cat inside especially during hot weather. Older automatic garage doors can crush a cat.

Cats given the run of the outdoors can encounter unneutered cats roaming the neighborhood. If your female cat is not spayed, expect regular pregnancies. Each year thousands of unwanted kittens are destroyed in a sad testament to such carelessness. An unneutered male will inevitably get into cat fights, and even a neutered cat can be the victim. Cat bites often abscess and result in costly vet visits, but encounters with other outdoor cats also carry graver dangers—rabies, feline immunodeficiency virus (FIV), feline leukemia, and infectious peritonitis. Any of these can be contracted through bites or other direct contact with bodily secretions, and several have no cure.

Indoor cats are safe from outdoor predators such as coyotes, owls, and even dogs.

Though you may think a cat can easily outmaneuver a dog, over any distance a dog usually wins. Packs of dogs pose a particular danger. Coyotes, more common in many urban areas than people realize, routinely hunt and devour outdoor house cats. Meanwhile, as cats do their own hunting, they can catch diseases, including rabies, carried by rodents. This is especially true of cats who have not been vaccinated.

If your pet can get outdoors, she is bound to encounter people other than those in your household. Some people just don't like cats or, even if they do, may well resent having their flower beds used as litter boxes or the wild birds in their yards stalked and killed. If your pet is bothering the neighbors, it is you, not your cat, who is irresponsible. Don't expect your neighbor to speak to you about a problem; many people feel they are entirely within their rights to trap, poison, or even shoot an animal trespassing on their property. Children are another danger. Though outright abuse is rare in most neighborhoods, children sometimes pick on animals, even an obvious pet, for teasing or worse.

So with all of the dangers to be faced outside these days, why take a chance with your feline friend? Cats adapt easily to life indoors, especially if they are raised inside from the time they are kittens. People tend to overestimate a cat's space requirements, which are actually quite modest. And though cats certainly need exercise, they can get plenty even in a small apartment. As long as you provide a lot of toys, take the time to play and interact with your cat, provide a good scratching post, and take your cat on a walk from time to time, your friend is sure to stay active and limber. An indoor cat can be trained to honor household dos and don'ts, remains unchallenged in his private domain, and, perhaps best of all, is always around for you to enjoy. If, however, you're out of the house for most of the day, a second cat may be a good idea. Constant feline companionship offers endless opportunities for activity.

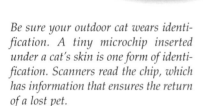

Be sure your outdoor cat wears identification. A tiny microchip inserted under a cat's skin is one form of identification. Scanners read the chip, which has information that ensures the return of a lost pet.

Cat Proofing

Do not overlook the hazards that may lie in wait in your own home. Once your cat gets comfortable in his new surroundings (and you want this to happen sooner rather than later), much exploration will ensue—especially if you have a normally irrepressible, globally curious kitten. Boundless energy will focus on investigating every nook and cranny, so it's up to you to ensure that those nooks and crannies are safe. Remember that we have taken cats out of their natural environment for our own delight and are thus all the more obligated to protect them from dangers that do not automatically register to them as such.

Get down on your hands and knees, and take in your home from a kitten's perspective. Do electrical cords from appliances or lamps temptingly dangle, challenging a young pouncer and inviting a crash from above? Can the wires themselves be chewed upon, risking electrical shock? Tape all cords and wires down, or tuck them away out of sight, to secure the area. If you use an electric blanket, your cat may favor being near it when it's in use; make sure there is ample protective material around the wires, particularly if your cat decides to knead it. Get used to closing toilet lids. Kittens can fall in all too easily, with dire results.

Keep sharp objects such as pins or nails, razors, scissors, and knives—all of which can twinkle irresistibly to a kitten ready for action—out of your cat's reach. Likewise, cats are attracted to the kind of cellophane wrapped around cigarettes and candy boxes; once ingested, it takes on the characteristics of glass and can slice into an animal's insides. Even Christmas tree tinsel and angel hair can lead to intestinal obstructions or internal cuts—in fact, many such seasonal celebratory accessories can wreak havoc on a cat's system, from the poinsettias

Keep an eye on Kitty during birthdays and holidays. Ribbons, bows, and even some foods can choke, poison, or injure a cat who may find these items irresistible.

on your table to small geegaws on wrapped presents to snippets of ribbon to the water your tree may be sitting in. If you are considering giving a holiday gift of a kitten or cat to someone you know who wants one and is ready to take on the responsibility, by all means wait until the height of the season has passed and the household has returned to normal. It is unfair to all concerned to introduce a new creature to the frantic pace, commotion, and distraction of the holidays.

Cats love small objects and, unfortunately, have been known to swallow them. So keep a tight lid on your sewing basket, and survey your surroundings with a critical eye for rubber bands, string, ribbon, thread, beads, buttons, and bells. And that classic ball of yarn? Unless you are there eyeing the proceedings, an enthusiastic cat could start ingesting the seemingly never-ending strand. Because cats virtually cannot spit anything out (that's how their tongues are constructed), by the time their system induces vomiting, the offending matter may be too deeply lodged.

Cats can finagle their way through the tiniest of openings.

A high-spirited kitten or even an adult cat can burrow, slither, noodle, and otherwise ingratiate himself through or into just about any closet, cubicle, or cabinet. Keep tabs on your new arrival so he doesn't slip out through a small hole in the screen door or inadvertently get locked away. And speaking of locked: Many a new owner has left a kitten in a bathroom or kitchen to return minutes later to find that the animal has, for all intents and purposes, vanished. One person finally unearthed her tiny cat from the lower mechanical innards of the fridge; another waited a whole day for his kitten's emergence from behind the cabinetry in the bathroom. There have also been reports of kittens getting trapped in the fridge itself, not to mention in closets, drawers, ovens, and clothes washers and dryers.

Be aware of accessible windows, too, even ones open "just a tad." Cats can squeeze themselves into the tiniest spaces, and if those spaces lead to a small ledge over a great height, the results can be tragic. Yes, cats can walk a pretty straight line and traverse the top of a fence or a mantel, but their sense of balance is not infallible. What lures them out onto the sill in the first place—a fly, a bird, an intoxicating scent, the flora in a window box—can further distract them once they've gotten outside. And though cats have traditionally displayed competence in keeping their balance in trees, remember that a cat can dig his claws better into a tree than a windowsill. Even a ground-floor window can beckon a curious kitty out to a world in which he is not prepared to survive.

Poisons That Lurk

Do you have houseplants? Most coexist with cats uneventfully, but some are poisonous and have to be put well out of an ardent young explorer's nibbling reach (and nibble they will). To be sure that your greenery is cat safe, consult a veterinarian, nursery, or poison control center. Meanwhile, a product called Bitter Apple can be sprayed on your plants without harming them and will discourage feline gourmets.

Some Poisonous Houseplants

- Dieffenbachia
- Philodendron
- Chrysanthemum
- Azalea
- Berries
  (Holly, Mistletoe)

Some Safe Houseplants

- Swedish ivy
- Coleus
- African violets
- Ferns
- Spider plants
- Palms

Be sure the plants you keep around the house are safe for your feline nibbler.

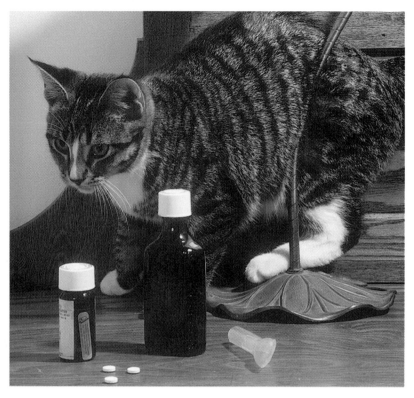

Cat-proof packaging? For safety's sake, keep all medications locked in a drawer or cabinet.

Medications are other everyday household items that could be toxic to a cat. Consider the medications you use and perhaps keep in plain sight, on a counter, sink, or nightstand. Even over-the-counter drugs can pose lethal consequences to a curious cat. Stow them safely out of reach.

What about those cabinets under the sink in kitchen and bathroom? If a toddler can get into them, an ambitious feline can, too. The contents awaiting there are often deadly, especially anything with the chemical phenol in it. Remember, even a small amount of oven cleaner or drain opener can do grave damage, so secure your cabinets to keep cats out. Beware the usual child proofing: Those locks that allow cabinets to open just a couple of inches provide enough squeeze-through space for a kitten with investigation on the agenda. Rubber bands may prove effective, though you must be vigilant in rewinding them around cabinet knobs and handles when you've closed the doors.

While it is unusual for cats to actually ingest a poison directly, they sometimes get toxins on their feet or fur and then become sick after they groom themselves. Insecticides and rat killers probably account for the majority of cat poison cases, so if you need an exterminator, find one who'll use sprays that don't harm pets. Strange as it may seem, the taste of antifreeze is exquisitely attractive to a cat, and it is all too easy to overlook a small pool of it under a car in the garage—until your kitten feasts on it with deadly results. Don't overlook mothballs, which also come under the "small objects" heading. They roll, they're bite-size, and they're lethal.

Finally, make sure your garbage is inaccessible, or at least tightly sealed or protected by a latching top. An errant chicken bone, for instance, can too easily lodge in a kitten's throat, with grievous consequences. Even the string from a roast can entice and cause harm.

Toys

The best way to assure the safety of a young creature so motivated to explore, pounce, jump, grab, swat, and chase is either to join in with the play yourself or to provide plenty of attention-grabbing, parent-approved playthings. Again, be

Your cat's favorite toys may be anything that includes you.

cautious and use your common sense: cute thingies that dangle on a string, say, are fine if you're there to oversee how they're used, but the small parts can get swallowed, and the string can tangle in a throat or wrap itself around a small neck. Provide toys that cannot be chewed into pieces or swallowed.

But before you start shopping at the nearest kitty boutique, remember that some of the best and safest toys are usually right at hand. Most cats seem to prefer those that are light enough to travel distances with minimal effort, as well as those that are soft enough to sink sharp claws and teeth into for grappling and pouncing.

Try an open paper bag (never plastic) or cardboard box on the floor, and sit back while your cat investigates it. Stack a few boxes atop one another for a more interesting terrain, and

Some of the best kitty toys are right at hand.

change them every few days to keep up the challenge and vary the environment. Wrapping paper and newspaper—tented, precrinkled, or rolled into a ball—are timeless favorites you can also enjoy as you watch your cat attack hidden objects and

Simple, Parent-Approved Toys

- Ping-Pong ball
- Knotted or rolled-up sock
- Crumpled paper
- Walnut in its shell
- Bottle cap
- Plastic lid from bottled water
- Cardboard toilet paper roll
- Twisted pipe cleaner
- Empty spool
- Pencil
- Pen cap
- Wine cork
- Catnip mouse
- Drinking straw
- Leaves from a celery stalk
- Light from flashlight or reflected off a mirror
- Grapes
- Shoelace (especially dragged across the floor by you)

think he's the stealth kitty stalking other pets while his behind and tail poking out the back of tented paper give him away.

Other favorites include aluminum foil, hard rubber balls (too large to swallow, of course), and that other classic, the ball of yarn (but only if you're there to supervise). Some owners claim the perfect distraction is a simple feather duster. But don't presume your cat will respond instantly to his new toys. Kittens are, after all, individuals, and one's object of bliss might be another's instrument of tedium. Be patient; it shouldn't be too long before you hit upon something absorbing.

One last word about cat toys: A longtime cat expert has found that recycling her cat's toys serves the same purpose it did when she recycled her children's. So when the thrill is gone and a toy seems to have lost its immediate appeal, whisk it away for several weeks—after which it will be new all over again.

Nothing is more relaxing than watching a cat sleep—other than cuddling with a warm, furry, purring cat yourself.

Beds

Finally, think about where and on what you want your new pet to sleep. The kind of bed you choose may well become a destination and retreat for a cat's fifteen to sixteen hours a day of naps, curl-up times, and longer, more serious sessions. A nice high-sided plastic bed with washable bedding or a beanbag bed that conforms to the body are both favorites. The tried-and-true (and much less expensive) lined cardboard box with high, draft-resistant sides and cutout entrance is also a good choice. Baskets look charming, but they are not easy to clean and are too easy for fleas to get comfortable in and around. Be prepared, however, once having thought everything through, for your new companion to select his own favorite destination on a couch, chair, floor near a heater, or on your very own bed.

Your Cat Comes Home

6

I t's official: You have a cat! Introductions are all-important. Start things off on the right foot, and you'll save yourself wear and tear and sleepless nights. Above all, take your time, and give the gift of patience to your new pet. Rushing things will only prolong the adjustment.

To begin with, you may want to confine a new kitten to a small area for the first two or three weeks, especially if no one is home during the day to oversee things. This will minimize the potential for mischief and maximize opportunities to introduce discipline in the most positive way. Then acquaint your new kitten gradually with the rest of the house. If other cats or dogs have been living with you, keep them away from their new roommate for the first two weeks until the kitten gets secure in her surroundings—and until you have visited the veterinarian for a checkup to confirm that she has no diseases.

You will likely be getting your kitten at her most significant time for developing social behavior—between eight and fourteen weeks of age. During this period, the relationships she establishes and the social behavior patterns that set in will greatly affect your kitten's future personality and determine how she adjusts to life with people, other cats, and other animals. The more gentle, pleasant experiences she has with people and other pets during this time, the more likely she is to become friendly and strongly attached to you, your family, and your friends. Without these early, enjoyable experiences, your kitten may develop into an aloof, wary creature—the sort that cat cynics associate with the stereotype of independent, uppity felines.

This may also be a good time to introduce your kitten to different environments—always gently and with sensitivity, of course. Short, pleasant car trips and visits to new, safe places encourage the blossoming of a more adaptable cat. The earlier you start, the greater your chances of success. With this in mind, do not force a kitten into situations if she is fearful; this only worsens the fear.

Introducing the Newcomer to Other Household Pets

Do not expect your current pets to organize a housewarming party for your new kitten. Resident indoor cats may greet a young newcomer with hisses, growls, and even a swat or two—it's their territory, after all, that has been invaded; and all those cooing noises and gentle attentions you may shower on

Your cat will adjust to the addition of a kitten much more easily than she would adjust to the presence of an adult cat.

the interloper probably don't help either. Remember, too, that an indoor cat who has spent her life without feline companionship may never have seen another cat since leaving the litter—an event long forgotten. An advancing kitten who is rebuffed will most likely retreat, then try again in a while. How things progress depends on the personalities involved. Sooner or later a truce will enforce itself.

The week before a newcomer arrives, spend extra time with your resident cat to instill a sense of security. Then once it's time for acquaintances to be made, the following scenario is recommended by many vets and behaviorists. Before the arrival, make sure that both the resident cat and the newcomer have had a delicious meal. Then have a person outside the family bring the kitten (in a carrying case) in for the first time (and only once the cat has been found to be disease free). Leave the case casually without comment for the resident cat to investigate on her own while the humans conduct a visit supposedly unrelated to any feline occurrences. After fifteen minutes or so (you really have to play this one by ear) the family friend opens the case, and the people end up (oh, so casually) in another room. This leaves resident and newcomer to sniff each other out more fully and without human scrutiny or interference. Hissing, a normal, defensive reaction, should be ignored, as should chasing (especially if the roles are exchanged occasionally) as well as any other complaints—short of screaming and loud growling.

Once the two cats stop pacing and settle down, the people should leave the house for half an hour or so, then return to resume their conversation, continuing to ignore the cats. The visitor then departs, conveniently forgetting to take his cat with him. Thus begins the gradual process of the new cat's absorption into the household, with as little fuss made over her as possible and many indications that your first cat remains the favored one—all this to foster a strong bond between the cats.

Another approach for when such an elaborate ruse cannot be arranged is to keep a new cat in a separate room for a two-week period. If there are no airborne diseases present, the established cats and the newcomer can make their acquaintance by sniffing one another out along the bottom of the closed door during the "waiting period." Then, when introductions are appropriate, keep the other pets away until your new cat has had a chance to explore her new surroundings, and closely supervise the first encounters. Consider putting up a baby gate or playpen to allow for further investigation without intimacy, especially when you are unable to closely supervise. Try to avoid showing favoritism, and be generous with affection to all concerned.

Keeping a new cat in a separate room for a couple of weeks will help your cats get used to each other.

Simple common sense dictates that most cuddling, holding, and reassuring of the new cat take place out of the field of vision of any resident cat, though the new cat's scent on you will attest to your ministrations. Extra time set aside in which to reassure old-timers will pay off in the end. It is to everyone's benefit that the newcomer be embraced, and that all parties eventually become fast friends. However new and older cats interact, do not force the issue, and try not to hold either cat in your arms during those first series of encounters. Aside from the favoritism implied, you may be leaving yourself open to scratches inflicted by an animal who suddenly and emphatically determines to be somewhere else—fast.

Cats have their own ways of establishing hierarchies, with eventual order and peacefulness as a goal. If things persistently look grim in the beginning, separate the warring parties for a few hours (a sudden loud noise usually surprises them into stopping their mayhem long enough for you to put a sturdy box or wastebasket over the aggressor while you remove the victim from the room). Then let down the barriers. Observe, but keep your cool, even if a loud fuss erupts at first. Settling in may take some time, but it is almost sure to occur. And once it does, the bond that forms and strengthens only encourages serenity, security, and the affability quotient in your home.

This adult cat has welcomed a young kitten into the family.

How to Introduce Yourself to a New Cat

🐾 Extend your hand toward the cat's face, about a foot away.

🐾 Look at the cat briefly, and then turn away. (Do not stare.)

🐾 Speak calmly. Say the cat's name. Make pleasant conversation.

🐾 If the cat withdraws, stop the interchange and your overtures.

🐾 When advances resume, slowly and calmly stroke under her chin and jaw.

🐾 Take your time.

How to Pick Up a Cat

Contrary to what you might have observed a mother cat doing to her newborns, never pick up a kitten or cat solely by the loose skin at the scruff of the neck—mother cats use their teeth in a special way that is not easily replicated by humans. Instead, support a cat in such a way as to make her feel safe.

Most important is to use two hands when picking up a cat, supporting the belly and the hindquarters, taking care not to squeeze too hard. A kitten can be scooped up from underneath and cradled in the palm of one hand while the fingers of the other gently support the head, under the neck. An older cat can be lightly gripped at the scruff but support-

Above: *Kittens must be fully supported by two loving hands when someone picks them up.*

Teaching a Child to Safely Hold a Cat

Cats are actually vulnerable and easily injured if dropped or mishandled. One way to get around a child too young to safely carry a kitten is to have the youngster sit on the floor and let the kitten come to him or her. That way the child can pet the kitten safely, and the kitten can retain some autonomy. But such an arrangement won't work for all youngsters, especially toddlers, who are too young to either understand their strength or control their impulses, no matter how kindhearted they may be.

ed on the backside, the cat's heaviest part, with the other hand. Another way is to hold the cat with one hand under the rump, and use the other hand to support (but not hold) her front paws.

If you want to be especially civilized and respectful and win your cat's everlasting trust and undying devotion, first make your intentions known, and then have her face away from you before picking her up. And as a final bow to etiquette, do not breathe into the cat's ears, eyes, or nose; it's as uncomfortable and ticklish to the cat as it would be to you.

Where and When to Eat

Some cats just can't resist water from the faucet.

Find a place to feed your kitten that is out of the general flow of commerce in your house, perhaps in a corner of the kitchen. It's best if there is a regular feeding area where a small creature can dine in peace. To this end, put a mat, tray, or newspaper beneath the feeder to catch spills, and keep the area clean.

Fresh water should always be available, but don't be surprised if your cat waits awhile before drinking it—or goes to a "stale" pool elsewhere. Chemicals in treated tap water can prove intolerable to a cat's highly developed sense of smell; with time, the worst of it fades as the water sits. But cats are quite individual in their preferences: some prefer bottled water, others like to drink water flowing from the tap. It's best to pay attention to your cat's behavior and go with the flow (forgive us) with this one.

As for solid foods, current knowledge indicates that the best way to feed your cat is in several small installments throughout the day. This healthier alternative to leaving food out insures that the food gets eaten. If you leave a larger portion of food out for your cat, it can last for hours and go bad, crust over, attract bugs, or lead to overeating. Smaller allotments also more closely replicate the eating rhythms and portions of a cat in the wild who hunts small prey such as mice. And speaking of small mice, try to make sure a kitten's food is at room, if not mouse, temperature. Some cats throw up their food if it's too cold, and others may ignore cold food altogether, because they aren't able to smell it.

Each cat should have her own food bowl not only to prevent fights but to prevent the passage of germs as well.

Put in your kitten's bowl the appropriate fraction of the daily ration recommended by your veterinarian (each pet should have a separate dish), and let the kitten eat for fifteen to thirty minutes. After this time, remove any remaining food until the next meal. You can add any uneaten equivalent to the next feeding.

As the kitten gets older (or as your schedule demands), you may choose to cut down on feedings per day, but no fewer than two daily feedings are recommended. A kitten on a diet of canned food especially needs more frequent feedings. Canned products are high in moisture and low in calories, making it unlikely that a kitten will get enough nutrients in one feeding to meet her needs. Such food also spoils if left out for too long.

Many experts recommend giving your cat fresh vegetables on a regular basis. Outdoor cats fill this need by chewing weeds, grass, and other plants, while indoor cats may be prompted to sample houseplants or cut flowers to satisfy the urge. Cooking bite-size green and yellow vegetables and mixing them into food every few days should discourage any inappropriate exhibitions of completely appropriate cravings.

Satisfy your cat's craving for fresh greens by chopping up kitty-sized portions of green and yellow vegetables.

Watch to see that your kitten is growing the way she should. If you can easily feel her ribs under the skin but cannot see them, that's a good sign. And use your common sense; if your cat seems a little fat, then she probably is a little fat.

Foods to Avoid

- Raw egg whites

- Anything with bones

- Raw fish (destroys vitamin B_1)

- Raw meat (can carry parasites)

- Dog food (doesn't provide necessary nutrients)

- Spicy foods (bad for the stomach)

- Milk (can cause diarrhea in some cats)

Using a spray bottle for discipline can be an effective and harmless way of deterring your cat from unsafe or destructive behavior.

As for just when mealtimes should occur: Be prepared for any young cat worth the pads on her paws to awaken at dawn and importune you for breakfast. Urgently. Insistently. To a supreme, tuneless symphony of yowls. If you know what is good for you, you will, early in the game, disregard each and every one of those soul-destroying sounds and make it a habit not to feed your cat until you're ready. If you leave the house every morning, feed your cat right before you go out. This will reduce the stress of your leaving, associating it with the longed-for meal, and will also buy you some morning time in bed. As another way to allay your cat's urgency, offer less glamorous dry food in the morning, and save canned food for the evening.

Basic Training

When it comes to introducing your cat to the rules of the house, the prevailing wisdom echoes current advice for teaching children: emphasize the positive. Negative corrections—shouting, whacking, chasing, heaving—are discouraged, not only because they are inhumane and cruel, but because they simply don't work. This said, many cat experts advocate a squirt bottle to be used immediately at the time of destructive behavior. Because the cat does not associate the spray of water with you—she associates it with the action that brought the water on—she does not come to fear you. Some breeders and other cat professionals suggest keeping many spray bottles throughout your home as a means of reinforcing house rules. Being sensitive, intelligent creatures, cats learn fast.

Two other tools of the trade operate on the principles of surprise (as in making a sudden loud noise with a whistle or crashing pan) or disgust (leaving an odor known to be offensive to cats, such as citrus, in an area to discourage a cat from leaving yet another unwelcome deposit in that very place).

But why not prevent undesirable behavior before it starts? You can head off the most common problems by getting the right start during kittenhood with meals, a clean litter box, a scratching post, and even toys.

Where a Cat Should Scratch

Cats were made to scratch, and scratch they will. It's that simple. They scratch for several reasons: to mark territory by leaving both a scent and visual mark for other cats; for claw maintenance; to stretch muscles and tendons; and to play, especially when they're kittens. Set yourselves up—you and your cat—for success by encouraging the cat to scratch items meant for that purpose, as opposed to the new sofa or a favorite easy chair a frisky feline may take a shine to if left to her own devices.

A scratching post protects your furniture and carpet by providing an important outlet for scratching. A post wrapped in a coarse, rough-textured material such as sisal and one that has a solid, square base is particularly appreciated. One scratching post is good, but two are better. Try, if you can, to get an upright post for climbing and stretching vertically and get a horizontal mate to provide a choice. Place them where your cat spends most of her time—where she sleeps, where there is action, or near windows or doors where she might see other cats outside, invading her territory.

Soft, vertical objects are often sought after for scratching, and once a cat has shown a preference for a certain surface such as

This Burmese uses a scratching post, making potentially destructive behavior acceptable.

the arm of a chair or a drapery it can be difficult to break the habit. One solution may be to make the object of desire less attractive, perhaps by sheathing it in thick plastic—some cats hate plastic—or another fabric sufficiently different in texture from the original. Then put a scratching post in that very area, preferably covered with fabric similar to the damaged one the cat was scratching. Nubby materials that allow for claws pulling in and out are usually appreciated, as is sisal. Toys dangling from the post or the scent of catnip may provide even more incentive.

Litter Box Behavior and Misbehavior

When a kitten is a month old, she is ready to eliminate into loose, soft, particulate material, so by the time she makes her way into your life, be sure there's a litter box nearby, kept very clean, stocked with litter the cat is familiar with.

Place the litter box in a safe, quiet spot so your cat can concentrate on business in private.

Kittens seem to have a natural instinct that leads them to use the box and to bury their wastes. Should this behavior not display itself, there is usually some reason other than not knowing how. Therefore, holding a kitten down in the box and moving her paws back and forth will not teach her anything but to associate the box with unpleasant times, and possibly even frighten her. Perhaps the litter is strange or different, or maybe the location of the box is simply too public—remember, a cat using the litter box is in an extremely vulnerable position and requires some privacy.

Once a cat has been trained, deviations from acceptable behavior usually indicate a medical problem, such as a urinary infection, and should prompt a call to the veterinarian. But if there is no such condition, then consider other issues: Has the litter box itself been kept very clean? Is it located too close to the cat's food and water? Is there an appliance nearby that makes a frightening noise? Could other household pets be interfering with business? Is the covered box too confining or the pan liners a turnoff?

As you're working on correcting the problem, thoroughly clean the soiled areas outside of the litter box to make sure your cat does not return to those places. Neutralize the odor with a mixture of vinegar and water. Never use an ammonia-based cleanser, which will only set the smell you're trying to

Hot Tips for Litter

- Baking soda sprinkled in the box is a good odor absorber and is usually undetectable to cats.

- Cleansers often leave a residue of scent in the box that cats will avoid, so rinse thoroughly.

- If your plastic box seems to attract stains and smells, try a disposable liner, or switch to a stainless steel pan.

- If a cat claws through litter liner, put folded newspaper sections over the liner.

- To control scattered litter, put a plastic grass doormat right by the box to help divest paws of residual effects.

eliminate. If these measures do not adequately discourage unwanted behavior, then reinforce the area in question with a scent known to be loathsome to cats—floral room deodorizer, menthol, or anything with a strong citrus odor.

Keep in mind that cats often have an agenda beyond mere elimination: urine marking, or spraying, is an important means of feline communication with other cats—and with people as well. (It is no fault of theirs that we cannot appreciate their messages.) "I was here," it can indicate, or "Keep away." Unneutered males are the most outspoken in this regard, though their altered brethren—male and female—often have their say as well, especially when having territorial issues with other cats in the household, or even with a cat spied through a door or window.

Changes in routine can cause litter box misbehaviors. The arrival of a new baby may set off alarms to a sensitive cat, who may respond in confusion to the new routines and household bustle by regressing to pre–litter box days. The cat also may be taking cues from the odor of the baby's diaper, which sends a message that this is acceptable behavior. Sometimes a normally fastidious cat may leave her urine or stool in inappropriate places when a new pet appears on the scene. She is confirming her place and position in the family, since leaving feces in a conspicuous place is a sign of dominance. Or perhaps there has been some territorial disruption, as when the house is being enlarged or remodeled and the new addition—considered foreign or outdoor—is thus treated accordingly. Finally, a bereft or devoted cat may leave unwelcome deposits on personal items belonging to a household member who has been gone a long time—offerings that may seem intended (much like Hansel and Gretel's bread crumb trail) to mark the departed's way back home.

It's true: Certain canny owners have managed to train their cats to make their deposits where the rest of the family does. Read up on toilet training before attempting it, though. It takes time, a lot of patience, and nothing's guaranteed, but there are at least two techniques that have been known to work. The success of this exercise in behavior modification depends on your cat's inherent attitude toward change and especially on your own commitment and forbearance.

Playtime!

Few things are harder to resist than that small, responsive ball of fur straining to pounce, leap, hurtle, and wrestle with you. Her tiny sharp teeth and claws hardly register if they sink into your skin, and what fun it is to engage so energetically, so wholeheartedly, so intimately.

But before you establish such rough-and-tumble routines, remember that soon this powerhouse of sweet scampiness will grow into an animal meant to survive and hunt in the wild, and those darling pounces will have sharp claws at the end of them, and teeth that could do some real damage will have developed. Your cat, meanwhile, will still want to "play." So when a kitten is being kittenish, resist the temptation to indulge and play rough. Make it clear that no part of your body is a toy. Distract your cat with suitable, interactive toys she can attack to her heart's content—chances are she will go for nearly anything that moves. Prevent bad habits by discouraging the cat from going after you or other people.

Should your cat nonetheless develop wild and crazy behaviors, or if you've inherited a grown cat with such inclinations, resist the impulse to "fight back," even in fun, and instead try making a sudden loud noise or blow on a whistle—or if necessary revert to the squirt bottle—to signal that this is not acceptable behavior. Remember, cats may be domesticated, but we have not succeeded in utterly bending them to our will (thank goodness); their rambunctiousness is normal and healthy, and it is up to us to channel those predatory actions into suitable outlets.

If, however, there is true aggression—if your cat is clearly bent on doing harm—a real problem may exist. The cat may be ill, in pain, afraid, or threatened, or may even be redirecting aggression toward you that is actually meant for another animal. Aggression is a serious matter, so consult a veterinarian about this. The solution may lie in a consultation with a certified behavior specialist. Yes, there are such people, and their experience and counsel can be infinitely helpful for those times when all else seems to have failed.

Where (and When) to Sleep

Sleep. Get used to it. Your cat will be indulging in some form of it much of the day—as in up to sixteen hours (maybe even more), many of them in the form of catnaps—and in the least likely places. But your cat will no doubt have certain requirements for serious sleeping: places that are warm, quiet, and not too bright. Often these spots turn out to be with you or another pet, despite the lovely bed you may have prepared and carefully outfitted. Even if you're charmed by the idea of a feline sharing your bed, you may eventually, in the interests of sanity and a good night's sleep, regret the consequences—often exhibited in nocturnal bounding, stampeding, galloping, zooming, batting, and general carrying on. By then it may be too late for much behavior modification. So if you are so inclined, lay down some rules while your kitten is still young.

Cats spend most of their days sleeping.

Before your own bedtime, enforce a routine by giving your kitten a snack, putting her in her own bed (warm and cozy, perhaps with a covered hot-water bottle), shutting off the light, and closing the door to her "bedroom," making sure she has litter box and water nearby. There will be protests (remember, she may be lonely without her littermates, may have done some heavy-duty napping during the day, and is, after all, nocturnal), but things will settle down in a week or so. Giving in, meanwhile, will only ensure you have a permanent, and perhaps not always welcome, bedmate.

Your Cat's Health

7

E ven if your cat enjoys a long and extremely healthy life, you need a veterinarian at hand for necessary inoculations, advice on health issues, spaying or neutering, grooming, and unanticipated emergencies. Next to you, the veterinarian is the most important person in your cat's life, so give your choice some thought.

Choosing a Veterinarian

These days practices range from multidoctor hospitals with specialists and state-of-the-art equipment to traveling clinics. Decide what is most important to you before searching for a vet. Is proximity to your home a factor? In other words, will you be less likely to follow up on care if getting your cat to the vet is a trek? Is cost an issue? You can shop around by calling and asking what office visit charges are or how much you'd have to pay to, say, neuter your tom. Consider, too, what services may be provided apart from veterinary care; many facilities now offer grooming, boarding, supplies, and food—one-stop cat care, so to speak—which can greatly simplify life for people whose schedules are on overload. Finally, determine how important it is to have an ongoing relationship with your vet, or what you expect to find in the tone and feel of the staff—brisk and highly organized, or nurturing and friendly?

You're now ready to consult your yellow pages and any other cat owners—friends, family, neighbors, breeders, coworkers—for names of veterinarians in your general area. Which places provide consistency of

Finding a Cat-Only Clinic

The American Association of Feline Practitioners (AAFP) can refer you to a veterinarian in your area who specializes in treating cats. Send a self-addressed, stamped envelope to the AAFP, 7007 Wyoming N.E., Suite E-3, Albuquerque, NM 87109; Attention: Referral Information.

care? Which will take you quickly if necessary, or have facilities suited to your needs? Is there a "cat only" clinic nearby? Do any vets make house calls? Local veterinary associations can be helpful in locating a practice that specializes in a particular area (surgery, internal medicine, neurology, dermatology, and so on) or that serves special needs you or your cat may have. Since not all veterinarians especially like handling cats, try to choose a practice with a sizable feline clientele.

As you get a better idea of what you expect from a vet and what your priorities are, you'll be better able to start narrowing the field. You'll want to visit those vets who have made it to the short list. Call to make an appointment if you want a tour or if you're interested in actually meeting the doctor. There's nothing to prevent you from stopping by on your own, however, to get a glimpse of the practice informally.

Try to get a feel for the philosophy of the practice concerning preventive versus crisis management, outpatient versus full service, and general options for client education. Is a doctor available to answer questions over the telephone? What are the

Choosing a Veterinary Office

There are many questions to ask yourself when choosing a veterinarian:

- How are the people out front, and how does the place feel to you?

- Does the staff really seem to care about animals?

- Is the place spotlessly clean, and are examining tables sterilized after each patient (some of whom may be highly contagious)?

- What are the veterinarian's credentials?

- Does the vet own a cat?

If this is your first pet, ask the person at the front desk what you can expect during the first year and what it is likely to cost. The kind of response you get—keeping in mind that the staff may be busy—will tell you a lot about how the office is run.

office hours, and how do they work with your own schedule? Finally, ask what kind of emergency care is available, either on the premises or at a central emergency facility.

Communicating with Your Veterinarian

Once you have chosen a vet, write down any questions you may have before your cat's first—and any subsequent—visit. It's a good idea to take notes on what you're told while you're there. (You may want to keep a "growth" notebook, charting progress and development for this purpose.) This may be a good time to think about how you would most like to receive

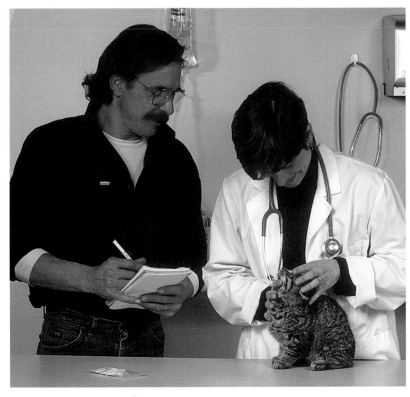

Taking notes while you're at the vet's office helps you keep track of your kitten's medical history and vaccination schedules.

information—through reading? hearing? doing? Letting your vet know what works best for you will lead to better communication through written literature, verbal instructions, or models.

If the vet prescribes medication, be sure you understand exactly why your cat needs it, how to administer it, and what, if any, side effects you can expect. Should any other home treatment be prescribed that you are not familiar with—administering subcutaneous fluids such as insulin, for example—be sure your vet or a technician shows you how it's done. Practice a few times while one of them is watching before leaving the office.

Do not be intimidated by any medical lingo you may not understand. Even well-intentioned vets can neglect to "say it in English" but will translate when asked.

Vaccinations

Not so long ago, cat care consisted essentially of keeping one's pet fed and loved. Medical attention and trips to the vet were reserved for the rare emergency, illness, or customary neutering. But medical care has evolved, and now most veterinarians' programs focus on preventive care, thanks to the availability of vaccines against diseases that may strike even indoor cats. So whether you get your cat from a breeder, a store, a friend, or a shelter, your first obligation is to ensure that he is immunized.

Vaccinating your cat is important not only to your own cat's health but also to the well-being of the entire feline community.

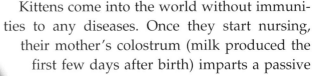

Kittens come into the world without immunities to any diseases. Once they start nursing, their mother's colostrum (milk produced the first few days after birth) imparts a passive immunity to any disease she has immunities to. This immunity neutralizes not only infectious agents in the kittens but also any vaccines they may have been given, making them ineffective for that time.

When kittens are between two and three months old, however, this early passive immunity decreases, enabling them to develop an appropriate immune response to a vaccine, which will protect them against that disease. Because the exact age at which this takes place differs from kitten to kitten, vets vaccinate frequently to be certain that protection has been achieved.

The protocol for certain vaccinations can vary among practices, so consult your veterinarian as to when, if, and how often to inoculate your kitten. In the meantime, familiarize yourself with the "alphabet soup" of the four primary vaccinations that are largely recommended for the diseases that follow.

The vaccine FVRCP or FVRCP-C (3-in-1 or 4-in-1) prevents cats from contracting feline distemper, feline viral rhinotracheitis, feline calicivirus, and *chlamydia psittaci.*

Feline distemper, or feline panleukopenia, is a highly contagious viral disease that causes fever, appetite loss, vomiting,

Feline Leukemia Virus

The deadly feline leukemia virus represents the leading cause of feline death in the United States. The good news is that the virus itself is susceptible to heat, ultraviolet light, drying, alcohol, detergents, and bleach, making it unlikely for your cat to get this disease unless he has direct contact with an infected cat's blood, saliva, urine, or stool (as in licking, biting, or grooming another cat or sharing food dishes or litter boxes), or if his mother was carrying the virus. Cats who are carriers often do not display signs of the illness but nonetheless shed the virus, so great care should be taken to test any new cat before he comes into your household, lest he infect your other cats. This disease greatly undermines the immune system, making an afflicted cat more susceptible to bacterial, viral, and fungal infections.

Whether your cat spends time outside or has any chance whatsoever of coming into contact with other cats—even through screened porches or doors, or a first-floor window—the FeLV vaccine is highly recommended; the consequences are simply too dire to take any chances.

diarrhea, dehydration, and other complications that frequently result in death.

Feline viral rhinotracheitis, or FVR, and Feline calicivirus are the most widespread upper respiratory viruses to plague cats. They cause fever, discharge from eyes and nose, and other nasty symptoms. FVR can lead to cornea ulcerations, cause blindness, or rupture the eye. As with the previous diseases, there is no cure, and recovered cats become carriers for life.

Chlamydia psittaci, covered by the final C in FVRCP-C, is also extremely contagious, especially in kittens. While it is rarely fatal, it can cause severe distress in the form of swelling and redness of the tissues around the eyes, and excessive tearing, sneezing, salivation, and coughing.

Cats are susceptible to other viruses as well. All birds and mammals are capable of contracting rabies, an ancient viral disease spread through saliva via bites, but some animals are more susceptible than others—cats being one of them. Widespread rabies regulation programs for dogs have decreased incidence of this disease for that species, but a combination of less stringent regulations and a great increase in the number of strays has resulted in cats being the most commonly infected pet in this country.

All cats should be vaccinated against rabies. Unlike humans, cats do not have the option of postexposure vaccines; none exist. If your cat gets rabies, he will die. If you get rabies and forgo postexposure vaccines, you may die as well.

Until recently, there was no vaccine or cure for feline infectious peritonitis (FIP), the second leading infectious killer of cats in the United States, and so little was ever mentioned about the deadly disease. Now that a vaccine (administered via nose drops) has been developed, we're hearing more about how the FIP virus is shed in the saliva, urine, and feces of infected cats, resulting in fever, weight loss, depression, fluid accumulation in body cavities, and most likely death. Your veterinarian will be able to advise you further about this and any other vaccines that may have been developed recently.

This cat is being vaccinated for FIP.

Spaying and Neutering

As many as twelve million pets are euthanized yearly in the United States simply because they're unwanted. Twelve million. Destroyed because there were no homes for them. This alone would be reason enough for every responsible cat owner to make sure his or her pet does not reproduce. But there are other, more tangible arguments to spay or neuter, and they all add up to a happier, healthier, more devoted pet, and a better all-around relationship for the two of you.

Some owners, understandably besotted with their pet, yearn for the creation of even cuter, fluffier, tinier versions of their beloved animal in the certainty that homes can be found. But the truth is, even if homes are waiting, how can these owners be sure that each and every one of those homes has a responsible nurturer ready to take on fifteen years of care? How can owners be certain that each and every one of those caretakers will spay or neuter that kitten? And if the kitten is not spayed or neutered, how can owners make sure that no doors or windows are inadvertently left open to provide a sexually active and determined cat access to his or her dearest wish? Any kittens born from such a midnight prowl, then, would ultimately be the responsibility of the person who encouraged that first litter. Meanwhile, those homes awaiting new kittens could have saved the lives of already existing kittens who otherwise may have been destroyed.

Millions of homeless cats are euthanized every year. Neutering your cat will help lower the death toll.

Cat overpopulation in this country has reached such a critical mass that even breeders and catteries are likely to include a spay and neuter clause in contracts, withhold registration papers, or register kittens "not for breeding" to induce new

Animal shelters are overflowing with homeless cats.

owners to alter their cats. So unless your kitten is show quality or in a professional breeding program, consider yourself obligated to do your part in controlling the spread of unwanted animals.

Dispelling the Myths About Neutering

Many misconceptions about neutering have proliferated, and neither cats nor their owners benefit from them. Contrary to myth, neutering does not deprive your cat of the chance to "fall in love." Cats live very much in the moment, and they seek a mate only when their glands tell them to. They mate and fight on instinct, not for the experience or to seek fulfillment. The same holds true for mothering impulses. Sexual cravings or the need to mother never cross the mind of a neutered cat, and research indicates that females who have been spayed before sexual maturity show no distress at having been spayed. But the many complications associated with mating (a rough-and-tumble affair for cats of both sexes) and the dangers and trials of pregnancy and birth can have a great, and not so positive, impact on a pet's life.

You probably won't make money selling kittens.

Cats do not necessarily get all lumpy and lazy and fat after being fixed. It's eating too much food that makes cats overweight or lethargic, not neutering or spaying. An altered cat's caloric needs decrease by about one-third, it is true, yet proper diet and exercise (and that can mean playtime) will keep your pet trim and in shape.

As for the surgery itself being dangerous, although no surgery should be taken lightly, neutering and spaying are such common procedures that veterinarians have become very good at them. Moreover, with the safer anesthetics now available, risks are decreased even further, and cats are back to their old selves within twenty-four hours.

Fixing your cat will change his or her behavior most definitely. But the changes are almost certain to be for the better. To understand just how much better, consider the behavior of unaltered cats.

Behavior of Unaltered Cats

Unneutered male cats spend a great deal of their time and energy trying to discharge their procreative obligations. Capable of breeding anytime, they are driven to seek out females in heat and to fight bitterly any other males similarly inclined. To this end, they aggressively mark their territory—including in and around your house—with an unmistakable, pungent-smelling urine, and wander far from home, often returning battle scarred and remaining just as restless. Should you succeed in confining a male cat, his frustration will express itself in heightened aggressiveness at home.

Unneutered male cats can wander far from home in search of a mate. If you don't neuter your female, be prepared to deal with howling suitors.

Female cats who have not been spayed go in and out of heat, or estrus, during breeding season, which can start in January and last until October. Cats kept indoors may go in and out of estrus all year long. A female in heat yowls and howls her yearning, rubbing against anything she can find, raising her hindquarters in the air with tail to the side and back feet kneading in desperation, rolling and writhing unceremoniously on the floor, and marking objects with urine to alert any

males to her condition. Overwhelming need may drive her to escape outdoors—despite your best efforts to keep her in—where she becomes vulnerable to getting pregnant, lost, or hurt. She is likely to become high-strung, jumpy, and nervous during these times of estrus, with diminished resistance to disease from the general drain on her body. There is also a likelihood that her unfertilized eggs, which do not pass out of her body the way unfertilized human eggs do, will become encysted after several unresolved heats and result in cancerous tumors. Unspayed females often suffer tumors in the mammary glands. These behaviors and conditions continue until the cat becomes pregnant, the season ends, or she is spayed.

Neutering your pet will decrease that urge to fight.

Advantages to Neutering and Spaying

Altering your cat dramatically reduces and, in some instances, eliminates the worst of his aggressive, restless, objectionable, and aggravating behaviors and conditions. Besides that, reproductive surgery has a number of beneficial side effects.

Male cats who have been neutered not only stop spraying strong-smelling urine (the urine becomes less offensive, and a neutered cat is less likely to spray), but also fight less and roam less—so they have fewer injuries, abscesses, or encounters with cars and aggressive, disease-carrying animals. Castration also eliminates the risk of prostate disease as well as testicular infection and cancer.

Spayed females are put out of the misery of needing to copulate, removed from the dangers of mating and pregnancy (including the wandering involved in looking for love in all the wrong places), and are spared serious uterine infections and mammary cancer.

Knowing all this, you will want to arrange for reproductive surgery as early as possible. Recent research has indicated that cats ideally should be neutered before reaching sexual maturity in order to reap the most health benefits, avoid behavior problems, and most important, prevent unplanned pregnancies. Shelters have been known, in the interests of beating nature to the punch, to neuter six- to fourteen-week-old kittens with no increased risk to the cats' well-being.

Neutered pets make more loving companions to you and to each other.

While healthy male cats can be castrated at any time, experts recommend that the procedure take place prior to puberty to eliminate a tom's opportunities for sexual experiences and thus any sexual behavior that may carry over despite the surgery. Ideally, females should be spayed when they are not nursing or in heat, since the uterus and vessels are engorged at those times, increasing the risk of bleeding. Your veterinarian is the best resource for guidance about the best time to spay or neuter your kitten.

To decrease the risks of the anesthesia, veterinarians now recommend routine blood tests prior to surgery to determine the safest possible drug for your cat and to confirm the absence of inherited or congenital diseases that might endanger the animal under anesthesia.

Before surgery, you will be advised to withhold food and water for a time to prevent vomiting during anesthesia. Afterward, your cat will be kept at the clinic for at least a few hours, and possibly overnight, for monitoring and observation.

When your cat comes home, you'll be told to keep him or her calm. Good luck. Most kittens bounce back so quickly they couldn't care less that they just had surgery and are supremely uninterested in restrictions of any kind. Nonetheless, you'll need to watch the incision for signs of discharge or swelling and to check that females are not disturbing their stitches.

While intact cats will do nearly anything to procreate, they will lose that drive and will not miss what they do not know if neutered early in life. Once you understand this, you will also understand what veterinarians, breeders, cat rescuers, cat lovers, and cat owners have long held: spaying and neutering your cat is one of the kindest, most important, and most responsible steps you can take to guarantee your cat's long-term health and happiness.

Typical Health Concerns

Cats are adept at hiding sickness and pain; it's part of their makeup to compensate for problems as long as possible. This is why many conditions don't surface for a while and why it's important that when they finally do, you notice. Because you spend more time with your cat than any vet can, it is up to you to be attentive enough to notice when your pet seems "off" and to be able to articulate just how this manifests itself. Sometimes the only clue that your pet has a health problem is that he deviates from his routine. Cats are creatures of habit, so observe your cat's behavior, diet, elimination, and attitude. In addition to knowing your cat, it is nonetheless helpful to be aware of common illnesses and conditions to look out for at different times in a cat's life. That way, you'll be more likely to go for treatment before it becomes serious.

Even normal-seeming cats can carry internal parasites such as intestinal worms, the most common of which are roundworms, Coccidia, *Giardia*, and tapeworms. Each type of worm is different, and so are the medications for each. Some parasite species are potentially zoonotic (spreadable to humans), so good litter box hygiene is important.

Because internal parasites are so prevalent—they can come with fleas, other infected animals, or raw meat, including dead mice and birds—it is important to have the stool of any cat you bring into your home checked out by a vet. You should also isolate a new cat from other cats until you're certain of the stool sample results.

Some vets recommend neutering kittens as young as six to fourteen weeks old.

The More Common Cat Diseases and Their Symptoms

Anemia: Anemia is a decrease in red blood cells that results in the insufficient delivery of oxygen from the lungs to the rest of the body. It is characterized by listlessness, loss of appetite, pale mucous membranes, enlarged lymph nodes, rapid breathing, and rapid heart rate.

Hypoglycemia: In the state of hypoglycemia, a kitten's blood sugar level drops dangerously low, resulting in weakness, listlessness, disorientation, blindness, collapse, and even seizures.

Internal Parasites: A cat with internal parasites displays a host of symptoms such as lethargy, bloated stomach, diarrhea, a dull coat, weakness, or weight loss.

Respiratory Disease: Colds are a serious health condition in cats. Take your cat or kitten to the vet if she has symptoms such as conjunctivitis, fever, loss of appetite, sneezing, and runny eyes or nose.

Abdominal Distress: The signs of abdominal distress are colic, pain, restlessness, and vocalization.

Once known as bladder stones, lower urinary tract obstruction, LUTO, has afflicted a significant number of adult cats, particularly males. Ever since it was determined that high amounts of magnesium in the diet and acid in the urine were responsible for the struvite kind of stones, cat food manufacturers began formulating their foods accordingly. The incidence of those stones in cats eating commercial diets were dramatically reduced. But another type of stone, calcium oxalate stones, still persist, and some experts think increased protein and salt in commercial foods is partly responsible for this.

Any number of skin diseases and external parasites can make your cat uncomfortable and undermine his health. Ringworm is a fungal infection, technically termed dermatophytosis or dermatomycosis. It is potentially contagious to humans and other animals and can lie dormant for a long time before manifesting itself. It first appears as a small, scaly, ringlike rash, usually on the tips of the ears and around the nose and eyes. As it gets larger, the animal's hair falls out in that area. Incidence appears highest during the hottest months and in warm, humid climates. A vaccination has recently become available to treat the condition once it takes hold.

Fleas are fast-moving, tiny, parasitic insects that congregate around the head, neck, and base of a cat's tail. They lay innumerable eggs all over the crevices, carpet, and furniture of your house (not to mention where your cat sleeps), as well as outside. Watch for flea dirt—tiny, black, comma-shaped flea drop-pings—if you notice any of the following in your cat: excessive scratching, chewing, shedding, or bald areas (some even red-dened), maybe with flaking, crusting, scabbing, or even bleed-ing. Sometimes the tip-off is merely a scruffy, moth-eaten appearance to your cat's coat.

A cat who excessively grooms or bites himself may have fleas.

Kittens are especially prone to tiny mites that live and lay eggs inside the ear canals and cause extreme itching, inflam-mation, black discharge, and wax buildup. Infection of the ear canal may follow. An afflicted cat scratches and paws at his ears and shakes his head for relief, which is not forthcoming. Mites are contagious to other pets. Untreated, they can cause deafness and even death. Consult your veterinarian to confirm the diagnosis and prescribe medication, which will require your persistent application.

Unusual buildup of dirt in a cat's ears requires a trip to the vet.

Lice are another annoying parasite. These tiny pinhead-size parasites don't move around but bury themselves in the skin. Cats bite their skin to relieve the itch. Flea powders or sprays are usually effective.

Tooth and gum problems such as red gums, bad breath, and difficulty in eating can signal dental and periodontal disease, and this in turn can lead to tooth loss. Dental plaque accumulates, irritating gum tissue and inviting bacteria. Teeth should be examined annually by a vet and

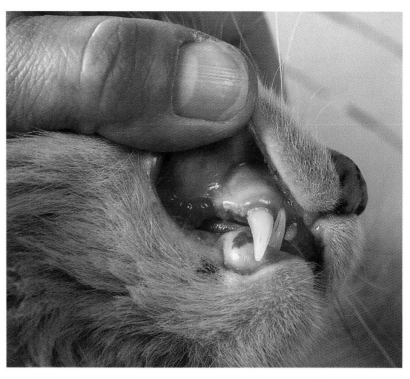

This cat suffers from periodontal disease, which is avoidable with proper dental care.

Suffering from an upper respiratory infection, this sick kitten also has a bloated stomach. Following proper vaccination schedules can help prevent such illnesses.

cleaned regularly at home with a soft brush and baking soda. Vitamin C may also be recommended.

Cats, like people, can suffer from upper respiratory diseases. But what causes mild "colds" in adult cats can produce severe and even fatal symptoms in a kitten, especially one younger than three months. Young cats living in shelters and multicat homes are particularly vulnerable to the two viruses responsible for most upper respiratory infections, or URDs. Although vaccinations against these viruses are available and in wide use, a certain level of infection is maintained in the cat population at large. This is because an overwhelming majority of recovered cats become carriers, capable of reinfecting any susceptible feline, particularly in such gathering places as kennels, pet shops, cat shows, or even usually clean and sterile veterinary clinics and catteries. All it takes is one sneeze from an afflicted cat, or contact with an afflicted cat in the form of grooming, food or water bowls, or even an owner's hands.

The best form of prevention is a well-maintained vaccintion

Symptoms that Require a Call to the Vet

- Loss of appetite
- Listlessness, depression
- Weakness
- Repeated vomiting
- Diarrhea
- Blood in urine
- Dehydration (skin doesn't spring back when pinched)

- Pale gums and tongue
- Red or swollen gums, bad breath
- Breakdown in personal hygiene
- Excessive thirst
- Hiding (sick cats often want privacy)
- Inability to urinate or defecate

- Rapid or slow breathing
- Pawing at ears
- Persistent scratching or biting of the skin
- Coughing
- Trembling
- Dull, patchy coat
- Limping for more than forty-eight hours

program. Beyond that, be sure to isolate any new kitten or cat for at least two weeks; by then, any signs of incipient disease will be evident.

In the course of your lives together, you are likely to observe a certain amount of vomiting and diarrhea. Vomiting is fairly common, given the cat's short alimentary canal, or digestive tract, and any number of nonthreatening things can bring it on: hair balls, food that's too hot or cold, eating too much food too quickly, or a sudden scare. Persistent vomiting can be dangerous and usually indicates a greater problem in the body such as poisoning, drug reactions, or disease. Likewise, a single episode of diarrhea may be the body's way, as with humans, of cleaning out a particular toxin, but anything more than that warrants attention.

Kittens cannot tolerate even moderate bouts of diarrhea the way grown cats can; they are likely to become dehydrated, and that can be deadly. Get help immediately for a young cat with diarrhea that has lasted more than six hours.

Call your vet, too, if your kitten suffers from prolonged, repeated, or projectile vomiting or dry heaves, and be ready to offer additional information—symptoms like listlessness or behavior deviations, as well as diet and what you may have noticed in the expelled material (food, hair balls, string, white foam, blood). As best you can, determine how often the bouts take place and whether they occur before or after eating.

Older Cats

Cats in their golden years are prone to many of the same problems and conditions of their younger compadres, but as with kittens (and, in fact, very old and very young humans), they have a lower tolerance for body stresses than more robust cats in their prime. So what may be an uncomfortable but non-threatening episode of, say, diarrhea for a two year old could

With vaccinations, dental care, and regular visits to the veterinarian, cats are living longer, healthier lives.

quickly turn serious for a thirteen year old. Keep this in mind when monitoring your aging feline. And to be safe, plan to take any cat twelve years or older to the vet twice a year for check-ups.

Cats, like humans, can be prone to constipation later in life. Persistent bouts of this common geriatric ailment can be serious, so consult your veterinarian. For occasional trouble, try offering a touch of milk, which is known to loosen things up.

Keep an eye out for hyperthyroidism, which occurs when a cat's thyroid gland produces excess hormones, causing the metabolism to speed up and affect other systems of the body. Muscles may weaken and atrophy, the heart may quicken, restlessness may set in. The first signs of this condition include weight loss despite increased appetite, great thirst, frequent urination, heat intolerance, bulkier stools, diarrhea, and vomiting. Fur may become matted, and claws may grow faster. A vet will suggest one of three treatments—medication, surgery, or radioactive iodine therapy. Because there is no known cause, there is no known prevention, but early detection can help in your cat's recovery.

When a cat suffers from chronic pancreatitis, the degenerating pancreas cannot produce enough enzymes to break down food. Despite a healthy appetite, your cat will have trouble maintaining his weight. You may notice vomiting between meals, a rough hair coat, and softer and lighter stools. Dietary supplements of pancreatic enzymes can help.

With an older cat, you'll want to be alert to any lumps that may appear on your cat's body. Lumps are fairly common in older cats and may be harmless. Tumors appear as lumps on a cat's body, but not all lumps are tumors. Tumors are a form of cancer, so any lumps found on your cat should be checked by your vet right away.

Older cats are susceptible to urinary problems, and most geriatric cats end up with some form of kidney disease. The kidneys, which filter wastes out of body, gradually deteriorate due to the burden of a lifetime of toxins in flea control products, insecticides, environmental contaminants, impurities, or

Pet Insurance

The best insurance you can provide for your cat is to keep up on all vaccinations and visit the veterinarian annually for a checkup. Beyond that, you might consider pet insurance, which is gradually becoming more available in this country. Veterinary Pet Insurance Co. (VPI) is a nationwide carrier that serves thirty-nine states. For around $100 a year, VPI offers catastrophic insurance to defray the high costs of treatment in the event of a pet's injury or illness. Deductibles range from $20 to $40, and there are discounts for multipet households. They'll honor a claim from any licensed veterinarian worldwide. For information, contact Veterinary Pet Insurance, 4175 E. La Palma Ave., #100, Anaheim, CA 92807-9903, or call (800) USA-PETS.

A few regional pet carriers have also sprung up, such as Manhattan-based Pet Assure and Medical Management International of Portland, Oregon, and there is every indication that this trend will continue as more pet owners seek out this service.

poor quality of protein in the diet. The resulting excess waste products retained by the body can cause a loss of appetite, vomiting, uremic poisoning, and even death. Cats with failing kidneys drink a lot (sometimes from toilets, sinks, or even fishbowls) and urinate frequently, lose their appetite or become more finicky eaters, vomit, and become subdued. Vets can give BUN (blood, urea, nitrogen) tests to determine the kidneys' function. Often large doses of vitamin C are recommended.

Psychological Distress

If suddenly deprived of attention and affection, cats of any age can become lonely and eventually depressed. They may stop eating and not take care of themselves. Some may even mutilate themselves when the situation becomes extreme—as when lost or abandoned cats get suddenly caged in an impersonal shelter or pound. Cats attached to other feline companions who die can suffer such grief that they stop eating.

And then there are those symptoms that coincide with changes in the household—a new pet, new baby, new home, or departure of a family member— resulting in a "sympathy lameness," wherein an animal will feign an injury to attract attention. Cats feeling neglected have been known to persist in holding up a front paw (sometimes the left, sometimes the right—they're clever, but not clever enough to keep track) to elicit attention from people they feel they've lost.

Cats confined to small spaces with not enough to distract them can develop stress symptoms—apathy, self-mutilation, loss of appetite, compulsive appetite—that a little more attention and stimulation may alleviate.

Psychological distress can also signal something physical. If your good-natured cat suddenly becomes ornery, chances are something's amiss. Remember, cats are so good at covering and coping with physical ailments that your first clue may be a change in attitude.

Cats need extra attention to feel secure and happy when their household goes though a major change.

Emergencies

No matter how careful you are, no matter how healthy—or lucky—your cat may be, accidents can happen. So be prepared. Few things can make you feel more helpless than watching a beloved pet going through sudden medical trouble and not having any idea what to do about it.

Learn to identify your cat's normal appearance and habits—the color of his gums, feel of his coat, look in his eyes, the way he walks. Can you tell if your cat's pulse is elevated (normal is from 160 to 240 beats a minute), or if he has a fever (over 100 to 103 degrees Fahrenheit, depending on your cat), or whether his breathing is irregular (outside 20 to 30 breaths per minute)? Your veterinarian can show you how to take these vital signs as well as how to perform feline CPR. The information may become invaluable one day. Beyond that, seek medical attention for anything that would prompt you to go to your own doctor were you to experience similar symptoms.

Keep emergency numbers close at hand—both the vet's and that of the closest emergency clinic, should your cat's vet not be on duty. And while you're at it, include the number for the nearest poison control center—you won't want to be tearing through the yellow pages just when your cat needs your concentrated attention.

A first aid kit is invaluable. Again, it helps to have everything together in one place for those times you may not want to waste a moment rooting around medicine cabinets or drawers. Keep a manual or first aid book in the same place.

First Aid Kit

- Round-tipped scissors
- Tweezers
- Gauze bandages (1-in. and 2-in. rolls)
- Gauze pads (3-in. squares)
- Cotton balls
- Rectal thermometer
- Medications
- Antibacterial ointment
- 3% hydrogen peroxide
- Milk of magnesia tablets
- Activated charcoal tablets
- Kaolin mixture
  Note: Administer milk of magnesia or kaolin only if specifically instructed to do so by poison control or your vet.

A first aid kit for your cat can prove invaluable in an emergency.

Cat Shows and Show Cats

8

When it comes to cat shows, there are those people who make pilgrimages to exhibit their prize pet, those who are curious about the latest in registered breeds, and those who thrill at seeing the winning specimen. Our suspicion, however, is that the real draw of these gatherings, aside from the glorious cats themselves, is the prospect of being with so many other people equally smitten with feline fever—of being with others of one's own kind.

Far from diluting the special and intense experience you may have with your own cat, shows somehow assure individual cat lovers that they're part of a greater, more inclusive movement. Everything that happens at a show and everyone who shows up has a real stake in a relationship with a cat. Every puss on display, every cage decoration, every new variety of kitty litter or scratching post or interactive toy on display is of interest, concern, and consequence at this convention of the converted.

The very first cat show was held in London's Crystal Palace in 1871, and since then owners have thronged to exhibit their cats for fun and to gain a reputation among other exhibitors and breeders. Today in the United States, local, regional, and national shows are scheduled year-round. There are four categories of competition: purebred kittens, purebred adults, purebred alters (neutered cats), and household pets (mixed breeds). Purebred cats are judged on temperament, health, and how well they fit their breed's official standard, while mixed-breed cats are judged on health, temperament, and general appearance. This last category tends to be the most popular with spectators.

Being There

Walking into a show hall for the first time may be confusing with all the different rings, which is where the judging takes place; and benching areas, which is where cats stay in their sometimes elaborately curtained cages between judgings.

Announcements peal over the loudspeakers, smatterings of applause crackle from clusters of onlookers at various rings where judging is taking place, and scores of people, with and without cats, stride purposefully in every direction. Meanwhile, there are catalogs and schedules to be consulted, plus booths selling the latest in cat care supplies and magazines, accoutrements, and adornments for the cat lover.

When it is time for a cat's class (breed and color) to be judged, the owner takes her to the appropriate judging ring,

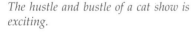

The hustle and bustle of a cat show is exciting.

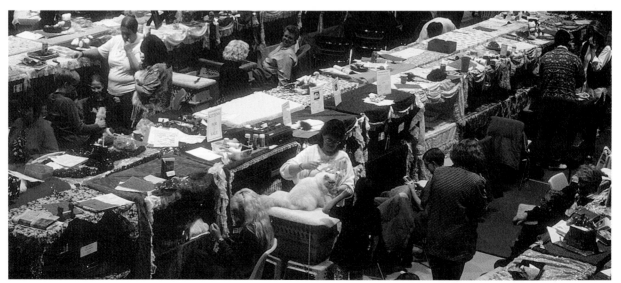

usually along the sides or ends of the hall for accessibility, and places her in a special judging cage. In turn, the judge takes each cat out of the cage, places him or her on the judging table, and examines the cat carefully, working with a judging book. This book notes each cat's age, sex, color, breed, and number and is where judges enter their "grades" or points. How well does the cat conform to the breed standards of perfection? Under scrutiny will be bone structure; coat and eye color; length of body, tail, legs; coat length; overall condition; and, of course, all-around health and degree of grooming. The cats are not named in the judging book so that each may be judged on his or her own merit. After judging each cat within a particular class or breed, preliminary awards are given (best of color, best of breed). Later, the very top awards (best all-breed kitten, say, or best of show) are meted out.

The judges are highly trained; they have bred and shown breeds of their own for years, have clocked in many hours in

What a winner! A woman proudly shows off her ribbon-winning Scottish fold.

various managerial capacities at cat shows, and have assisted other judges in show rings. In addition to that, they have been longtime members of at least one cat club and have exhibited extensive knowledge of all the breeds accepted for registration.

And the exhibitors? What's in it for them? Not monetary gain, for certain; cat prizes do not yield cash, and between entry fees and travel expenses, the tab for owning and showing a purebred can quickly add up. The draw, plain and simple, is a passion for the breed and a strong desire to be among those who share that passion.

What Is a Show Cat?

A show cat is not just any cat you take to a show. A show cat is a pedigreed animal who meets the requirements of the breed's written standard; this standard, set up by the cat registries, describes the perfect example of each breed and lists features that can disqualify inclusion. A show cat also must be a good traveler, put up with being in a show hall and cage for the weekend, and tolerate being handled by judges.

Show cats, such as this Russian blue, must put up with the judges handling, poking, and pulling them.

Pedigreed show cats are best purchased from breeders who themselves show cats. These breeders are not only likely to be reliable, they also have a reputation to uphold, having a track record in the show ring. But be prepared: any breeder with strong credentials will want to make sure you know what you're getting into and that you are prepared to follow through with not only the usual care and shots and grooming, but with the rigors and responsibilities of keeping your show cat in top condition. A breeder may even retain co-ownership of your cat and any control over offspring (this is a good thing; it helps assure that you select an appropriate mate).

Once you and a breeder decide which purebred will be yours and at what price, that breeder will present you with a purchase contract that provides a health guarantee, enumerates your responsibilities as an owner, and details what you can expect in the future from the breeder. He or she is bound to refer to a time in the future when you'll be sent your papers. These papers are proof that your cat is of known parentage and a pure form of a particular breed, likely to exhibit the traits of that breed. Those papers, usually a blue registration form, in turn get filled out by you and sent to the proper registry.

Purebred, remember, is not the same as having a pedigree, which is merely the written history of your kitten's parentage and could note the ancestry of a group of, say, barn cats. But when purebred and pedigree are combined, it means an ancestral history that shows that the parents, grandparents, and great-grandparents are known and pure for that breed. Lineage can thus be traced back to assure the breed has been maintained.

Your cat is registered when her name is entered into the books held by one of the cat associations your breeder is associated with, an association where your kitten's parents and grandparents and so on were also registered. The resulting registration papers reflect proof of ownership, breed, dam (mother) and sire (father), birth date, and that your cat's purity of breed and pedigree are recognized, accepted, and recorded by that cat association. The papers, then, represent legal documentation of who your kitten is and whom she owns.

After you have purchased your show cat, the relationship with your breeder may well continue as you rely on his or her advice and counsel. The breeder may even attend cat shows to track the progress of his or her very special progeny.

Make sure you get your cat's papers and health guarantee from the breeder.

The Six Major U. S. Cat Registries

Cat associations, or registries, keep records, sanction shows, select show judges, and charter clubs. They operate independently, not always agreeing on just how they define and treat breed standards and each having their own rules, but they are united in their commitment to keeping high bloodline standards, celebrating purebred cats, and promoting the welfare of all cats.

Registration rules used to be based on aesthetic rather than genetic tenets, but in the last twenty-five years or so, scientific breakthroughs have resulted in new, genetics-based registries, radically changing the way cats are looked at, shown, and registered. The International Cat Association, for example, is set up so that cats are registered genotypically (by their genetic makeup) but are shown phenotypically (by how they look).

If you would like information on the six U.S. cat registries, contact:

🐾 American Association of Cat Enthusiasts, P.O. Box 213, Pine Brooks, NJ 07055; (201) 335-6717

🐾 American Cat Association, 8101 Katherine Ave., Panorama City, CA 91402; (818) 781-5656 or fax (818) 781-5340

🐾 American Cat Fanciers' Association, P.O. Box 203, Point Lookout, MO 65726; (417) 334-5430

🐾 Cat Fanciers' Association, P.O. Box 1005, Manasquan, NJ 08736-0805; (908) 528-9797

🐾 Cat Fanciers' Federation, P.O. Box 661, Gratis, OH 45330; (513) 787-9009

🐾 The International Cat Association, 306 East Jackson, Harlingen, TX 78550; (210) 428-8046

Don't Forget to Have Fun!

9

Owning a cat is not all about studying and shopping and grooming and cat proofing and feeding and litter cleaning and inoculating—not by a head of whiskers. Once you've taken care of the necessaries, untold adventures and delights await you: a mass of fur draped and nestled around your neck, purring, and midnight coverlet ramblings, to name a few. Your cat is wild enough to provide hours of excitement as he stalks, ambushes, and pins down prey as varied as walnuts, pipe cleaners, or balls of yarn, and yet tame enough to clue into you in an instant to rub and twine himself ecstatically around your legs when you return home after an absence.

Cats are also very smart—smart enough not only to learn witty and amusing tricks but to deign to learn tricks only if doing so will further their immediate interests. This means they can learn them if they decide there's a reason to cooperate, and if they get the feeling they are working with you and not for you. And so, armed with patience and determination, a person can try to corral a cat's keen awareness of the world and get him to learn a trick or two.

You can teach your cat to roll over by using rewards. First, gently push your cat into a lying position saying "roll over." Immediately reward him. Then roll your cat over after giving the command,

Yes, cats can learn tricks, but it takes some patience on your part.

always rewarding the cat immediately with his favorite tidbit. Soon the command alone will suffice with the reward, of course, always given.

Some cats are naturals at fetching, while others never seem to get the hang of it. Try throwing a ball of paper and see if your cat goes to get it and bring it back to you. If he does, then throw the object again and make a pretty fuss if it's retrieved. It may take practice for both of you, and it may take a few sessions, but if your cat is of the retrieval ilk, you'll have a fun routine in place for the two of you.

Some tasks such as sitting up, on the other hand, require a slightly more sophisticated procedure. For this, professional animal trainers rely on shaping, which reinforces successive approximations or behaviors leading up to the final, desired one. A cat being trained to sit up is reinforced (with a small tidbit) first for sitting down, paws on the floor, in front of the trainer. After several repetitions, it's time for the next step: now the cat must lift a front paw off the ground to get the snack—something he might do naturally to get at the tidbit to begin with. When this behavior is duly established (tidbit offered the moment of the desired behavior), the requirement is changed again to include both paws being airborne before any tidbit is forthcoming. Only then is the command "sit up" invoked and from that time on repeated.

And speaking of rewards, a word here about catnip. This time-honored herb can inspire even the most laid-back cat to engage in the friskies. After treating your cat to a small dose, be sure to set aside some time to watch the show and to interact; your pet will be hot to trot—playing, exercising, and generally rolling around blissfully. (Some cats are highly sensitive to this stuff, so go easy at first.)

Enjoy your kitten's playfulness, and take plenty of pictures.

And for goodness sake, don't forget to take pictures! Lots of them. In the beginning, especially, be sure to buy extra film for your camera and take the opportunity to record the antics of your adorable, curious, stampeding, cuddly, sometimes deranged Marco Polo; you will be glad you did, because in just a few months that very same animal will metamorphose into a more stately, dignified, and serene adult bearing little resem-

Cats enjoy sharing every aspect of your life.

blance to the tiny, enchanting, and maddening kitten who captivated your heart and took over your life. Now is the time to get your hands on a camcorder to record some of those timeless moments. You will never regret it.

Sometimes the greatest joys come, serendipitously, from those habits and idiosyncrasies that are of a particular cat's true nature, and not any person's whim. So take your cue from the charming and delightful traits your cat displays on his own, and encourage and respond to them. Whether your cat is lolling on the floor with belly exposed and paws curled under the chin, or reaching up to turn a doorknob, or watching a game on TV and batting at the action upside down from a perch atop the set, you probably have a host of entertainment options to choose from right under your very nose. And rewarding those behaviors that you find most enchanting or amusing—with exclamations, attention, or tidbits—will only serve to reinforce them.

For every year your out-of-control kitten seems to take off your life, you're sure to be compensated by the ample health benefits that same pet is bound to provide you. Scientists have found that stroking and petting a cat reduces stress and calms and relaxes one's entire system—so much so that hospital patients have shown dramatic improvement when allowed the friendly physical contact and steadying influence of a cat's company. And people with heart ailments have had blood pressure alleviated and stress reduced by developing an ongoing feline relationship. Maybe it's the fact that a cat is about the size of a human baby, or maybe it's the basic nonjudgmental nature of any relationship between human and cat. In any case, it's good for the soul, and it's good for the body.

Final Words

Watch, listen to, and always try to understand why your cat is doing what he's doing. You will not necessarily yield to all his demands or behavior, but you'll show respect for your pet. And in return for your respect will come your cat's trust, affection, and steadfast devotion—currency that remains, for all time, priceless and irreplaceable.

Glossary

bunting: rubbing or pushing with the head; cats bunt against other animals or objects to scent mark them

castration: removal of the testes or ovaries

colostrum: high-protein milk with a high content of antibodies that is produced during the first few days after a dam gives birth

dam: the mother of a litter

domesticate: to shape a species of animal over time to live with and assist humans

estrus: a recurrent state during which most female mammals are fertile; heat

juvenile phase: phase of a kitten's development, from fourteen weeks to the onset of sexual maturity, when established behaviors and skills become more refined, complete, and efficient

neonatal phase: first phase of a kitten's life that lasts for about ten days. It is marked by helplessness, dependence, and the need for nourishment and a mother's care

neuter: to castrate or alter a male or female cat

nictitating membrane: a thin protective membrane beneath the lower eyelid that can cover the eyeball

pedigree: an ancestral line of descent especially as diagrammed on a chart to show ancestral history, including parents' names, colors, and registration numbers

purebred: a cat bred from members of a recognized strain, without admixture of other blood, over many generations

queen: a mature female cat kept for breeding

quick: the pink part of a claw containing nerves and blood vessels, which you want to avoid while clipping a cat's claws

sire: the father of a litter

socialization phase: phase of a kitten's life, from two to fourteen weeks of age, during which social play and interaction begin and behavior patterns are established; imprint phase

spay: to surgically remove the ovaries of a female animal

taming: getting an individual animal accustomed to the presence of humans

tom: an unneutered male domestic cat

transition phase: phase of a kitten's life, around the second week, during which eyes open, teeth grow in, and the kitten undergoes rapid physical change

zoonotic: a type of disease that can be passed on from animals to humans

Index